Praise for *On the Gaze*

"In a personal narration that reads like a reflective literary diary, Adrianne Kalfopoulou's *On the Gaze* chronicles the situational everydayness of her lifeworld in Dubai. The optics encapsulate manifold perspectives interwoven with anecdotes from the fabric of the city's recent history, and oriented by analytic leitmotifs with Baudrillardian attunements. She depicts the intercultural arabesque of the cosmopolitanisms of a maritime megalopolis that rose in its architectonic edifices from the purity of the Arabian desert dunes. Dubai appears through her gazes as experiential labyrinthine lessons of inhabiting the locales of a global landmark of urbanity that reflect the neo-aesthetics of our hyperreal paradoxical age."

—**Nader El-Bizri**, author of
*The Phenomenological Quest
between Avicenna and Heidegger*

"Adrianne Kalfopoulou's *On the Gaze* is a book-length essay on her immersive experience upon entering, and living in, a world far from her own cultural roots. We follow her multiple gazes—temporal, abstract, theoretical, and personal—and journey with her through Dubai's humble beginnings as a port village to its evolution as a global city of the digital age. The book abounds in honest and vivid portraits of people and places written in beautifully crafted prose. A very welcome addition to the growing body of anglophone literature on the Arabian Gulf."

—**Yahya Haidar, editor and translator,**
*Al-Din: A Prolegomenon to the Study of
the History of Religions*

"Adrianne Kalfopoulou has created a conceptual and reflective astrolabe of Dubai that could well become the new intellectual way of entering its space. Her narrative slides effortlessly on the chronological map crossing the gaze of time with the tactility of experience—hers and those of many others who have found themselves in this place of futurity in the hopes of escaping the vicissitudes of their individual presents. Transnational fluidities, Kalfopoulou tells us, rest on narratives of a future that has already become another mirage. Infrastructure indexes forms of modernity, and on this conceptual map we see fixed points that sculpt the modernities of the Gulf States—the hospital, the airport, the bank, the gaze from above, and the vision to the future, in a narrative that is as detached as a surgeon's scalpel and as intimate as the literary account of a pedicure."

—**Neni Panourgiá, author of**
Dangerous Citizens: The Greek Left
and the Terror of the State

ON THE GAZE

The Speaker's Corner Books Series

Speaker's Corner Books is a series of book-length essays on important social, political, scientific, and cultural topics. Originally created in 2005, the series is inspired by Speakers' Corner in London's Hyde Park, a bastion of free speech and expression. The series is influenced by the legacy of Michel de Montaigne, who first raised the essay to an art form. The essence of the series is to promote lifelong learning, introducing the public to interesting and important topics through short essays, while highlighting the voices of contributors who have something significant and important to share with the world.

ON THE GAZE

DUBAI AND ITS
NEW COSMOPOLITANISMS

ADRIANNE KALFOPOULOU

Fulcrum Publishing
Wheat Ridge, Colorado

Library of Congress Cataloging-in-Publication Data

Names: Kalfopoulou, Adrianne, author.
Title: On the gaze : Dubai and its new cosmopolitanisms / Adrianne
    Kalfopoulou.
Description: Wheat Ridge, Colorado : Fulcrum Publishing, [2023] | Series:
    Speaker's corner | Includes bibliographical references.
Identifiers: LCCN 2022051767 (print) | LCCN 2022051768 (ebook) | ISBN
    9781682753460 (paperback) | ISBN 9781682753729 (ebook)
Subjects: LCSH: Cosmopolitanism--United Arab Emirates--Dubai. | Dubai
    (United Arab Emirates)--History. | BISAC: SOCIAL SCIENCE / Essays |
    SOCIAL SCIENCE / Sociology / Urban
Classification: LCC DS247.D78 K35 2023 (print) | LCC DS247.D78 (ebook) |
    DDC 306.095357--dc23/eng/20230124
LC record available at https://lccn.loc.gov/2022051767
LC ebook record available at https://lccn.loc.gov/2022051768

"All That We Have" by Khalid Albudoor is reprinted by
permission of the author.
Cover image is of the Dubai Frame, which stands in
Zabeel Park, Dubai.

Cover design by Kateri Kramer

Unless otherwise noted, all websites cited in endnotes
were current as of the initial edition of this book.

Printed in the United States
0 9 8 7 6 5 4 3 2 1

Fulcrum Publishing
3970 Youngfield Street
Wheat Ridge, Colorado 80033
(800) 992-2908 • (303) 277-1623
www.fulcrumbooks.com

For Lizzie Torres

Photo courtesy of the author.

PREFACE

All That We Have

Because no one is there
We will lie down
On the shoulder of a dune
Gazing silently
At colors of far hills
We wait for no one
You might say
No more Bedouins
They disappeared
All of them
Before we knew them
Or wrote their names
On the skins of our tent
Before we learned love from them
And I would say
Look carefully
Behind our dune
I can see their souls approach us
Rising from the mirage of distance
Or
Appearing to us from
The future.

Khalid Albudoor

Port towns are known for gathering people from different parts of the world, whether on small islands—I think of Greece's Syros—or the larger, famously known cities of old, such as Egypt's Alexandria, the port of Chittagong in Bangladesh, and Greece's Piraeus, which enabled the Ancients to defeat the Persians in the famous battle of Salamis in 480 BCE. China, too, since its ancient past, has been home to two of the world's largest ports, which today are in Shanghai and Shenzhen. All this to say that the ports of the Arabian Gulf have attracted traders from different continents for centuries, with the Dubai Creek being one of its hubs. Today, Dubai's Jebel Ali Port constitutes one of the world's largest harbors, after Shanghai, Rotterdam, and Hong Kong. I don't know that geography is destiny, but it certainly makes access to the world at large likely or less likely. That Homer's *Odyssey* traverses seas that connect peninsulas and coasts is no accident. Was this perhaps my interest in writing about Dubai, or what's come to be today's megalopolis city? I was interested in the desert as much as the port. The desert being a kind of tabula rasa for projections that trade in possibilities, a trade that the Dubai Creek harbor made possible in the early days of its development—in 1901 Sheikh Maktoum bin Hasher made the creek a free port with no taxation on imports or exports promising merchants protection and tolerance, as well as providing them with some land. As the Emirate poet Khalid Albudoor writes with some melancholy, "the mirage of distance" suggests both a lost Bedouin past as much as the possibility of a future—in this case, a future in which such loss may be more fully understood.

There was much I did not know when I first arrived in Dubai. In that, I was like so many. This essay is about that journey, both the fact of not-knowing as much as the fact that I found myself part of a larger question regarding what it means to live in liminal spaces; the "in-between"[1] as the postcolonial theorist Homi K. Bhabha puts it, is a space of "intersubjectivities" that deconstruct the ways we see within our specific (cultural) self-referentiality. Bhabha notes that "the overlap and displacement of domains of difference" in such in-betweens bring about a "disquiet-ing" but also potentially fertile encounter with the other. For Bhabha, the encounter with cultural difference is one of mutual disquiet and negotiation in which "one both abandons and assumes associations" (Bhabha 1941–2). As such, the gaze—how one looks upon the other—ruptures any neutrality of how our subjectivities come to bear on what we see. Having lived between cultures for most of my adult life—in Greece, for short stints in the United States, as well as Germany and Scotland for brief teaching assignments—perhaps I was already attuned to a sense of liminality, my own as much as the city's.

On one of my first days at the school in Dubai where I would be working, I was asked if I knew anyone in the city or region; when I said no, the answer seemed to surprise

HR, a Jordanian man who was helping me with onboarding. His expression seemed to recalibrate how smoothly I would acclimate myself. Friends and colleagues (in the States especially) were somewhat reserved about my decision to work in the UAE (United Arab Emirates). "How do you feel there, being a woman and on your own?" I didn't feel any more "disquiet" than I'd felt teaching in the United States, where racism was palpable and the dollar a craven deity. I was surprised to learn that several of my colleagues in Dubai left their apartment doors unlocked; in a region where 90 percent of the inhabitants are transplants, we become guests not only within the mores of our host country but also within the changing terrain of our personal subjectivities. I was interested in who gathers here. As strangers in a desert sharing unlikely common ground, we formed a community.

∾ • ∾

The spectacular skyscrapers of downtown Dubai are overt signifiers of the Gulf port's evolution from its 1930s and '50s status as an informal British protectorate state into an independent global metropolis of the UAE. When I arrive, I am driven to a development cluster in an area that, like much of the surrounding desert, keeps changing. Everywhere cranes perch like prehistoric birds atop rising structures at different heights, seemingly in the middle of nowhere. When I say, "What's that about?" to Lizzie, my young colleague, as we pass another glass and steel monolith with a scrim of trees at its base, she says, "It's just randomly there. . ." and adds, "I swear all these buildings could just as well be pitched tents in the desert." Ongoing construction projects have become the default signifier of Dubai's modernizing ethos. But what I see, too, is what remains relegated to private spheres, unavailable to the public gaze. Beauty salons whose doors and windows are papered over, posters of women having any number of beauty procedures cover them; popular images include eyebrows being shaped and lashes being extended. Door signs note explicitly that only "Ladies" can enter. There are contradictions in what I see, but maybe this is only specific to me. The papered-up windows and doors provide images to suggest the realities we don't see. Perhaps this is one way to read the spectacle that is Dubai: as a participatory fantasy we partake in from our different perspectives. How we look at objects, or the world more generally, becomes implicated in what we see. In other words, there is no such thing as a neutral gaze. This idea became increasingly important to me as I was immersed in the city's many visual fields.

The first time Lizzie introduced Mirosh, another colleague, and me to Arabian food, I noticed a woman in full covering, an abaya and niqab, eating at a table by herself. Only her eyes were visible, and they were focused on a large plate of meat and rice in front of her. She was carefully spooning the rice and cutting slices of meat off a bone as she lifted her veil and slipped a spoonful of food into her mouth, letting the veil fall over it as she chewed. I remarked that she was at a table alone in the busy restaurant where locals, and mostly families, were gathered. The servers weren't being any more attentive to her than to anyone else as she quietly ate her meal, seeming to be in no rush. I kept thinking the rice might spill because of the veil, that she would check her lap (things I'm certain I would have done), but her eyes stayed on her plate, occasionally looking up at nothing in particular. When she was done, her plate empty, she drank her tea before opening a purse to pay. Perhaps she'd been in the restaurant before; maybe this was more of a routine than I realized, her routine Saturday meal. "It's because she's in a place where there are men," Lizzie says, when I remark that it must be hard to eat with a veil. "If there had been a separate room for women, she would have taken off the niqab to eat."

Other space markers include areas in supermarkets selling pork; a sign in GRANDIOSE above a meat counter notes "Non-Muslims." I am as impressed that a space is made for non-Muslims who might want to buy pork as I am with the array of dates (SERRI, KHEDRI, JOMARA, KHATT, SAFAWI, DEGLET, and MEDJOOL, to name a few) and brands of rice. Basmati rice, for example, seemed already specific when I would look for it in European or American supermarkets. But when I go into LULU, a popular supermarket chain founded and owned by an Indian from Kerala, I see two aisles of rice in up to five-kilogram (eleven-pound) packets and count at least eight brands, including a nongluten version by TILDA. There's a Lal Qilla "Brown Basmati Rice" and a "Long Grain" version by Mubarak, an "Extra Long Grain" version by Qaswa, a "Pure Aromatic Well Cleaned White Long Grain Basmati" by Sinnara, and even a "Quick Cooking Brown Basmati Rice" by Daawat (which I bought).

What does all this say about my assumptions, assumptions implicated in any gaze? The variety of dates, like the variety of basmati, illustrated how little I knew of the culinary specificities of the region. It also revealed how reductive the terms "basmati rice" or "dates"—or beauty salons I could not see into from the street, and women eating in niqabs—had been to me. These were not one thing or one paradigm but rather a cosmos, a reckoning that began with my arrival.

I.

Pink neon contours a building at night. A near-empty walkway with a flashing monitor reads: "Dubai Digital Park." In the morning I see a concrete expanse of flat apartment rooftops amidst a humid, sand-infused horizon, the steaming heat of the desert temperature in August. Plasma screens along a walkway show scenes of people eating, exercising, shopping; these are the only people I see. I am in an area called Silicon Oasis. The name gives me pause. In his seminal essay "Simulacra and Simulations,"[2] Jean Baudrillard discusses "the dialectical capacity of representations as a visible and intelligible mediation of the real"; what is real here is as much a part of what I see on plasma screens in this Digital Park as the desert that surrounds it. Dubai, the city I've arrived in, built out of the desert, where 70 percent of the world is within an eight-hour plane flight from its airport, a geographical factuality of a crossroads between East and West. A city of spectacle and the spectacular, from its glass and steel high-rises, human-made oases, beach fronts, malls, free trade zones, clusters of micro-cities, and various Jumeirah (coastal residential) developments, is an image-making map of highly "instagramable" moments. From theme parks to commercial hubs, Dubai gathers people from around the globe and across the labor spectrum to serve and be served.

In the 2010 "UAE Vision Statement,"[3] Dubai's ruler, Sheikh Mohammed bin Rashid Al Maktoum of the Maktoum royal family, commits to making the UAE "among the best countries in the world" by the nation's 2021 Golden Jubilee. Sheikh bin Rashid Al Maktoum, Sheikh Mohammed's father, worked to make Dubai the cosmopolitan nexus it has become over a more than thirty-year period, from the 1950s into the late 1980s, when he suffered a stroke. Merging the visions of Sheikh Zayed bin Sultan Al Nahyan of Abu Dhabi, considered the UAE's founding father, with his own, Sheikh bin Rashid Al Maktoum is said to have looked toward the apparition of this new polis with "old Dubai" at his back. Today, "The Dubai Frame"—a steel, glass, and aluminum frame standing 150.24 meters (493 feet) high and 95.53 meters (313 feet) wide in Zabeel Park—represents the combined visions of Sheikh Rashid, Sheikh Zayed, and Sheikh Mohammed, Dubai's current ruler, to reflect the UAE's ever-modernizing potential.

It is instructive to contextualize today's proliferation of human-made lakes, beaches, and high-rises with the city's modest beginnings in the early twentieth century, when it was a port village of pearl divers and fishing merchants. Todd Reisz's meticulously researched *Showpiece City: How Architecture Made Dubai* (2021) has been my guide in charting the initially gradual, increasingly rapid, then dramatic changes that have led to the Gulf town's metamorphosis into a cosmopolitan city. As Reisz demonstrates, the recurring theme of "movement and transience" (34) were key influencing factors that continue to this day. A British outpost, by the mid-1950s the population of between 20,000 and 30,000 (according to British estimates) was "increasingly defined by its immigrants, or more accurately, by people passing through" (31). Arab, Iranian, and South Asian family-run businesses had learned to survive in "entrepôt"[4] fashion, a term used by the British Foreign office in the 1950s. As a port that both facilitated and profited by trade between places, Dubai's entrepôt location on Dubai Creek was both a fundamental ingredient of change and a key player in its survival. What began as a swampy port whose geography made for merchants who "learned to profit through the cracks of a fractured British policy," who "brought rice from Burma, wheat from Iran, flour from Australia . . . coffee from India and Yemen" (30–31), grew through stages of sometimes unlikely progress. As Reisz points out, "Dubai attracted trade, not because it was organized but because it was not" (34); with its imports and "re-exports" from Iran, India, and the African continent, there was a haphazardness and savvy to the manner of trade given the creek's location as "a quick, easy, and often dubious site for profit," where "a low-overhead profit scheme that required only the space and labor to move goods from one boat to the next or to storage in the souk" (34) made for lucrative business. A confluence of geography, acumen, and resilience would come to mark the standard for the port town's growth and its ruler's foresightedness.

Today, a tourist magnet and tax haven for the wealthy and wanted, a lure for those (like me) looking for salaried work that will let them save money, Dubai is, above all, seductive. Swaths of business intrapreneurs flock to its various "cities": Internet City, Festival City, International City, Sports City, and Academic City being some of the urban oases, like Silicon Oasis, that appear throughout the city's expanding parameters. Starting with "New Dubai" and its center in DIFC (Dubai International Financial Center), an ever-ambitious building-to-need culture has shaped the continuously changing desertscape and skyline. Optics, as much as economic necessity, have remained catalysts to this transformation. The roles played by Britain's political agents, people such as Peter Tripp,[5] were key. Tripp put forward the first organizational plan in the mid-1950s, highlighting the fact that "organizational clarity would bring optical clarity," founding, too, "the Trucial States" Development Office (TSDO), which initiated developing health care facilities, a vocational school, and irrigation and agricultural plans. Such "quantifiable, visible improvements" (44) served as the first steps toward a rudimentary infrastructure in a region once known as the "Pirate States."[6] Various treaties, beginning with the General

Maritime Treaty of 1820 that evolved into the 1892 exclu-
sivity agreement with the British, promised what became
known as "the Trucial States" military protection (thus
the term "British protectorate") against such powers as
Russia and France. The seven sheikhdoms on the Persian
Gulf and coast of Oman that made up the Trucial States
were Abu Dhabi, Ajman, Dubai, Ras al-Khaimah, Sharjah,
Fujairah, and Umm al Quwain (which would later form
the seven states of the UAE); each had separate treaties
with the United Kingdom that ensured a truce, hence the
Trucial States, for exclusive loyalty to Britain.

∺ • ∺

In November 1956, with Tripp's encouragement, the first
non-British, non-Western municipal advisor was hired by
Sheikh Rashid. Tripp advised that a consultant who was
neither British nor one from the powerful local majlis—a
gathering of merchants—who were increasingly suspicious of British influence (some of whom were connected
to the radical National Front[7]), should be hired. Abdul
Salam Er Raouf, an Iraqi from Baghdad, would serve as
consultant to help establish a *baladiya* (Arabic for municipality). Er Raouf's hire reflected the cultural interstices
of the British presence and Sheikh Rashid Al Maktoum's
gradually assertive role in the decision-making. Er Raouf,
who was associated with the Iraq Development Board
with its good number of British advisors, oversaw Iraqi oil-
funded infrastructure developments. The British Foreign

Office had to be convinced to pay for a non-British consultant and only came up with 3,000 rupees, while the rest of Er Raouf's expenses were covered by Sheikh Rashid; it was the beginning of loans that formed the basis of Sheikh Rashid's financial gamble on progressively ambitious infrastructure projects.

Abdul Salam Er Raouf's presence was both practical and symbolic; it expressed the growing—and lucrative—marriage of commercial interests with hybrid, or cosmopolitan, methods of cultural transaction. According to Tripp, Er Raouf was equally successful with the powerful merchants in the majlis as he was with the poor in persuading them to cooperate with such initiatives as public clean-ups of garbage. He brokered the establishment of an advisory group, the Dubai Council, and initiated fundamental requirements such as building permits and the need to have slaughterhouses "fly-wired" against insects. In short, Er Raouf's brief three-month stay garnered more local support and endorsement from the British Government than any British political agent up to that point. Most significantly, as Sheikh Rashid both hosted and paid for the bulk of his stay, it was also a turning point in attitudes toward the agency of the ruling family: "Presiding over the majlis with his Iraqi consultant by his side, it was now he [Sheikh Rashid] who instigated the making of the modern city that Tripp imagined" (53).

☙ • ☙

Throughout the gradual first steps of development of what is today's city was an ever-conscious, and self-conscious, understanding of the power of appearances: whether a municipal plan, film, architectural design, or today's spectacles—skydiving, sports parks, indoor ski slopes, to name a few—the projection of an expectation through an image of that expectation fed the potential for development. The signs, or optics, of what would constitute a developing town in and around Dubai Creek were reflected in Peter Tripp's 1958 promotional film *These Are the Trucial States*, funded by British Petroleum (BP). The film highlighted images of Dubai as an "urban crux" so that the other sheikhdoms might view it as a model to emulate. In creating a concrete, visual plan for infrastructure developments, as Todd Reisz has argued, Tripp assigned a quality of commitment and sense of permanence to what he envisioned. Through a constructed sense of permanence, with Dubai representing the more advanced sheikhdom of the region, Tripp's film scripted a fiction that enhanced images suggesting that anything outside Dubai's sphere belonged to a less sophisticated Arab world. As Reisz notes, "Idyllic shots characterize the other Trucial States in a supporting role. A shepherd steers goats from Sharjah to Dubai's markets, as if the hinterlands, not the port, feed the city" (56).

Seeking to garner financial support for Dubai's development, Tripp's 1958 film deliberately caters to the gaze of the British protectorate. In its black-and-white footage,

These Are the Trucial States does not distinguish between the Indian, Iranian, South Asian, African, and Arabic people who comprised the growing population. And as Reisz pointedly describes, "Someone with limited knowledge of the region might mistake them all as an indigenous people with a shared ethnic identity, working together to create a harmonious place" (56). In short, the "single comprehensible society" made out of an amalgam, or assemblage, of carefully picked images emphasized a town of work-intensive projects committed to permanent architectural and municipal structures. In Jean Baudrillard's discussion of simulations and the hyperreal, he suggests models of reality that are purely conceptual and boast no originating map. The hyperreal is a reality unto itself, more real than any reality that inspired it, a template, I would suggest, for understanding the spectacle that is today's city: "To simulate is to feign to have what one hasn't," writes Baudrillard, insisting that "to feign" is to en*act* that which *generates* a reality of its own; this is the hyperreal. It is what political agents such as Peter Tripp contributed to in scripting a narrative that created Dubai's emerging modernity.

One of the main obstacles to achieving that narrative lay in the source of the town's centuries-old livelihood, the port itself. Prey to the formation of sandbars and accumulated silt known as "silting-up" (a fate that all but closed down the Sharjah and Ras Al Khaimah ports), Dubai Creek was, according to an assessment by the British firm

Sir William Halcrow & Partners, in danger of deteriorating. The economic lifeline for Dubai also served British interests, so in 1954 Halcrow & Partners was hired to dig, clear, and deepen Dubai Creek to accommodate larger boats and facilitate trade. As with Tripp's *Trucial States*, William Halcrow's view on the port "documented the present for the sake of a future history—a history that Halcrow was prepared to author and profit from" (82).

William Halcrow's "Dubai Harbour Scheme" was ambitious and another savvy example navigating multiple cultural interests (and self-interests). The £388,000 Halcrow wanted to "rework less than a kilometer of Dubai over two years" (81) was not an amount the British Treasury was willing to pay, even though the Foreign Office expected to be "closely associated" with any infrastructure project. Like Tripp, who had encouraged Sheikh Rashid's hiring of Abdul Salam Er Raouf, the solution was to involve Sheikh Rashid more fully in financing Halcrow's engineering proposal by having him shoulder the entire debt. The aptly named "Harbour Scheme" was indeed a negotiating and strategic scheme that furthered Sheikh Rashid's agency as much as it added another mythmaking layer to this make-or-break moment in Dubai's narrative. The merchants' majlis backed the plan, as this was Dubai's primary trade connection to the world. With various proposals for financial support nixed, including one from the British Bank of the Middle East (BBME), linked as it was to the Petroleum Development of the Trucial Coast, who wished only to back "piers near their ad hoc exploration sites" (84), Sheikh Rashid signed what Reisz calls a "survival strategy" with the British government. Who controlled the money was not necessarily who controlled the narrative: if the British wished to script the narrative as seen in Tripp's black-and-white *Trucial States*, that Sheikh Rashid became the debtor to combined loans from the rulers of Kuwait, Qatar, and Bahrain added the ingredient of what "appeared to be" a British governmental project but was in fact negotiated within the context of regional powers. The British government was merely the broker, or in more contemporary jargon, the enhancer. They did also wish to be in a profit-making position were things to go well.

Peter Tripp was again an interlocutor. He choreographed Sheikh Rashid's debtor position, approached the majlis who agreed to help, and agreed to Sheikh Rashid's request that the British Foreign Office make the first contact with the emirs of Kuwait, Qatar, and Bahrain for a loan. The emirs from the other Gulf states would loan Dubai's sheikh money the British government would oversee. At Sheikh Rashid's request, British government agents contacted the emirs on his behalf. A loan of £400,000 was given to build the port's expansion, to be administered by BBME—it would receive a "handling fee"—and the risk was shouldered entirely by Sheikh Rashid. The government agents had become administrative bodies, or negotiating interlocutors, invested as they were in the potential of a more commercial port; they had nothing to lose, and every-thing to gain. British consultants and engineers would be well positioned to make profits, but the story of who dictated infrastructure initiatives in the Gulf town had shifted; Sheikh Rashid, through a debt "scheme" that involved the British government's administration, the endorsement of the majlis, and the backing of the emirs, became the person who gradually controlled, and by extension mandated, the potential of Dubai's future.

If a contractual mapping promised an actionable future for the Creek that would serve ever-larger ships with their cargos, it was a conceptual, even performative act that hedged the literally concrete hopes of the port town. As Baudrillard reminds us regarding abstractions in a hyper-real context, abstractions don't follow a map: they simulate realities. In February 1961, the work that Halcrow's harbor engineers had done had fallen prey to rainstorms and the shamal (sand-infused winds). The result was the clogging up of the port with a mixture of sand and debris, cutting it off from world trade. The British agent at the time, Tripp's successor Donald Hawley, who spoke fluent Arabic, found himself urgently negotiating between Sheikh Rashid (who paid his salary) and the Sheikh's British financial advisor, William Duff, who chose not to blame Halcrow's obvious miscalculations in his engineering of the Creek harbor's expanded concrete entry point. Instead, Duff recommended additional engineering projects to further expand and reinforce the harbor walls. This recommendation met, perhaps surprisingly, with agreement by Sheikh Rashid and the merchants, as both had experienced "a nearly 25 percent increase in imports, after prior years of single-digit growth" (90). In short, the returns on what the first expansion had garnered were proof enough that such projects brought profit. Profit had also been made by those British engineers whose engineering laid out the blueprints for ensuing works. "Halcrow's cost estimate for the next phases rose to £1,000,000 ($1,081,260) by 1964, nearly triple that of its first contract" (91); Halcrow also pursued other engineering initiatives such as the Al Maktoum Bridge, the town's first bridge and a sign of future expansion. Dubai's growth would move away from Dubai Creek—with its souks, open markets, hajjis, traders, and investors—toward an inland city.

∽ • ∽

In "What Is Cosmopolitan?" (2000), Jeremy Waldron distinguishes between the noun and the adjective forms of "cosmopolitan" to highlight "a way of being in the world," one that opposes "devotion" or "immersion" of or in a culture, as in a belonging by blood or faith. Waldron suggests the "cosmopolitan" is a person who does not associate themself "with any secure sense of place" (228). Underpinning this idea of the cosmopolitan is a questioning of permanence; broad swaths of populations—from refugees, itinerant workers, and nomadic populations to more sophisticated and consciously deliberate travelers—fit the category. Dubai's expression of cosmopolitanism begins with its history as a port town and a Trucial State whose vagaries of survival required the combined resilience of different bodies, a majority of whom were transplants and nonindigenous people. As the infrastructure developments expressed a British protectorate's wish to demonstrate organization and permanence, it was, somewhat ironically, a transient labor population who were building those markers of permanence. If more suspicious and less inviting of the British agents than the ruling Al Maktoum family, the local merchants acknowledged, and by extension supported, the infrastructure projects that were providing a better lifestyle: electricity, better hygiene, and most importantly clear profits as a result of the port's accelerated and further-reaching trade. For their part, the British continued their administrative oversight and profit-making investment in what Donald Hawley called the baladiya, using the Arabic word for municipality to emphasize that the English equivalent was yet to be achieved.

As Dubai's expanded port enriched trade, the engineering changes also reclaimed land around the creek, real estate that now belonged to the ruling Al Maktoum family. New housing projects, made of the concrete and steel that went into building the harbor, were replacing the wooden frames, palm fronds, and walls of limestone, coral, and mud traditionally used for homes. Somewhat alarmed by the rate at which growth was taking place, Donald Hawley urged Sheikh Rashid to hire a town planner who would make the potential of a real estate market at once measurable and lucrative. These first steps of a development plan are indicative of the ways Hawley, and then John Harris, Dubai's first town planner, directed, and helped shape, the ways Sheikh Rashid took ownership of his city. From the beginning, Hawley's view was to instill "a bureaucratic sensibility and an abstract appreciation of organization" (101), which included property boundaries as well as categorizing spaces with specific purposes. For example, there would be "classes" of housing as well as "plots" relegated to "mosques, clubs, petroleum sites, etc." (102). Any land without clear established ownership, according to these first measures, belonged to the Dubai government—in other words, the Maktoum ruler. For Hawley and others, this made the growing city-town legible, as it legitimized their projects, while simultaneously inducting Sheikh Rashid into the more cosmopolitan terms for pursuing, and leveraging, growth. With deeds that confirmed land ownership, owners could take out bank loans. Organization created legibility which in turn created legitimacy, albeit always in the eyes of those putting forward the templates.

John Harris was hired in 1959 to create a town plan when the population of Dubai was estimated to be around

40,000. At the time there was no existing "map," let alone a plan, for the town. Harris wanted an aerial photograph, which one Hunting Aerosurveys provided. Again, it was Sheikh Rashid and not the British government who paid the bill, and again it was the British government's need to ensure their distance from any potential liability (despite their ongoing oversight and hiring of key engineers like Harris) that caused delays. Interestingly, and somewhat prophetically, too, the aerial photographs mapped as much of what would become Dubai's potential as it did of empty space; the Hunting Aerosurveys map "makes no distinction between tentative structures and more substantial houses" (111). The observation somewhat eerily echoes the kind of cartographic surrealism of Baudrillard's notion of the hyperreal, a reality "more real" for its simulation of a potential: "It is the map that engenders the territory," he notes, a territory that expresses "vestiges . . . in the deserts which are no longer those of the Empire, but our own. The desert of the real itself." But for now, the desert, and the gaze upon it, fed not just those "vestiges . . . of the Empire" but also the reality of its desires as much as those of the kingdom's ruler.

In March 1960, John Harris received the completed map from Hunting, a facsimile of the existing Bur (an area of land) on which Harris sketched the lines of the new Dubai, or Bur Dubai; it would be measurable and follow a plan. The Al Maktoum Bridge would connect old Dubai, or

Deira, and the creek with the newer, expanding city. Importantly, unlike the intervention in Kuwait (again by British engineers), where the old city was razed (subsequently causing a hike in real estate prices that made housing unaffordable to the local population), Sheikh Rashid preferred a less risky intervention; the existing town would be gradually integrated with the new city. This ensured that trade would not be paused, and for the souks and the majlis who ran them, it would be business as usual. Sheikh Rashid's pragmatism, a middle-of-the-road approach, put forward that change "would mostly happen *by addition, not deletion*" (my emphasis). This approach of "augmented urbanism" passed no judgments on what came before it; there were "no assumptions that earlier development was insufficient or wrong; instead, it assumed that large-scale and technological advancement happened *beyond*" (118). This becomes a leitmotif of an ever-forward-looking investment that framed not only the Al Maktoum ruler's hopes, or vision—what the Dubai Frame today means to honor—but also the tenor and scale by which the foundational infrastructure of today's Dubai was created.

With the asphalt-surfaced roads of the "New Town Dubai" expanded to accommodate up to six traffic lanes, old Dubai's souks were busy with the increased business of new networks and of clientele, from the visitor who wanted tailor-made clothing to those seeking bargains of goods that were double or triple the price in Europe; modernization was taking place at different levels and at a different pace, depending on what part of the town one was engaged in. Certainly, the changes accentuated and accelerated what was already a characteristic of the port: the interchanges of culture. In his discussion of cosmopolitanism, Waldron points out differences between Immanuel Kant's notion of a "cosmopolitan right," defined as the jurisprudence of peoples sharing a world in which basic human rights are a kind of global rule of law, and a "cultural cosmopolitanism" that refers to whatever is not "single culture" and so is resistant to conflations with the global. In Waldron's words, it is cities like "New York, Paris, London and Bombay," and today's Dubai, that "are the urban centers of world culture; [because] they are great centers of trade, tourism and migration, where people and their traditions mingle and interact" (232). John Harris's town plan was foundational in laying the parameters and mapping for such interactions, from projects like the early Al Maktoum Hospital, to the creation of town squares such as "Cinema Square," where Deira's first outdoor cinema stood, to a tiered system of roads and roundabouts that connected newly formed and older Burs. Communities were forming that relied less directly on the harbor for business.

New Town Dubai included real estate projects on land reclaimed from the seafront. William Halcrow's expanded harbor had pushed the Dubai Creek's shoreline farther out. It was land that now belonged to the ruling family, and Sheikh Rashid had control of all development on it. Here buildings could climb a lot higher than the two-story limit in the rest of the town that accorded with Harris's town plan. As New Town Dubai grew according to Harris's map of neighborhood "units" that included amenities such as housing with plots of walled-in gardens, there were "property types"—larger, first-class houses of four or more rooms, and smaller, second-class houses. While there was no explicit reference to race, Harris's plan provided classes of housing that expressed the fact that those in cheaper housing were also doing the lesser-paid jobs and belonged to particular ethnic groups. As Todd Reisz notes,

> By 1965 there are only a few hundred whites living in Dubai. It could very well be that the plan did not antic-ipate that a large white population would ever need accommodating. By 1965, higher-paid Western families enjoy seaside villas outside the bounds of the town plan, as if they existed outside Dubai's cosmopolitan society. Most of Dubai's assembling middle class—immigrant Arabs and Asians—occupy the city's new neighborhood units, with informal segregation apparent through rent-ing and marketing practices. (125)

The British oversight—its gaze—on Dubai's develop-ment grouped communities by, among other things, their role in the growing labor force. If who was living where was not made explicit in Harris's housing plans, the regulation of space according to its function was, and this included those who lived farther out from the neighborhood clusters in a "lodging area" (126). Harris labels the increasing number of low-paid, mostly South Asian, workers who were entering Dubai the "migratory element," a term revealing for its bias on what was objectively the status of the majority of foreigners. "Element"—as opposed to, say, "community" or "peoples"—suggests both a detachment from and an ignorance of the reality that those migrants included individuals, like the British themselves, who were there to profit from work opportunities, albeit at drastically different levels of pay.

II.

I arrive in Dubai in August, and all I know of the city is what I see and feel. Like the burning surface of my skin when I leave the air-conditioning and move into the heated breeze of a late afternoon, surfaces are my indicator. They are also material, like the heat bearing down on me; the metal from my earrings singeing the flesh of my earlobes as I wait for a Careem taxi to pick me up after work. It is hard to stand for more than a few minutes in this temperature, and yet people work in it, itinerant workers mostly from South Asia, the Far East, and Africa. Colleagues keep urging me to rent a car, but the complicated roundabouts and ramps off and on Sheikh Zayed Road intimidate me, as does the fact that there are continuous works-in-progress that have any number of DETOUR signs. I know I would be overcome with anxiety, which has already become my default emotion. The driver who arrives is Indian or Pakistani. I've been told that the taxi drivers are generally from India or Pakistan, though it is local Emirates who generally own the companies. I notice other ethnicities in particular job categories. In the beauty salons it is mostly Philippine and Vietnamese women, and some African. Some salons have groups from particular towns or villages who come by word of mouth to share a work environment, like Ripa, who cuts my hair and is from Armenia. The cost of the ride to my rented apartment is twelve dirhams AED (3.2€ or US$3.26), the minimum charge. I'm told some years ago the minimum was as low as five dirhams. I see tasteful complexes of two-story villas blending into the sandstone shades of the desert, and in the distance the vague outline of other-worldly high-rises.

When I finally visit Downtown Dubai, it is night and the architectural spectacles of the city shimmer the skyline. The Burj Khalifa, at 829.8 meters (2,722 feet), scales the air as its thinning gradations of steel and glass peak in what looks like the needle of a syringe. I am thinking how Dubai does surfaces spectacularly and asking myself what it means for someone like me to arrive here without any sense of where I am beyond the markers of a job in a country far away from everything I know. There are light shows and fireworks over the human-made lakes and piers; the Burj Khalifa's height is splashed nightly in psychedelic colors and images, including that of its ruler, Sheikh Mohammed bin Rashid, projected along its sides. Watching the light shows and water fountain displays accompanied by music is a sensory immersion that gathers locals as much as tourists, which is as true of the malls and various beachfronts. I am among the privileged here. An educator. And my flat is being paid for by my employer. I don't live in a work camp, but I can see, in the building opposite mine, people living in shared quarters. Someone comes out on the small balcony and looks at himself in the sliding door's glass, which he is using as a mirror. He looks dressed for work, in a tie, and keeps combing his hair as he checks his reflection. Rows of shoes are being aired on a ledge. One morning I wake to men dangling from the rooftop, cleaning the building's glass siding; they are buoyed by ropes that hold them as they wipe the glass with extended mops. No one is white.

I am having a pedicure when Moon tells me she is going to be leaving Silicon Oasis because she got a better paying job at the Mall of Emirates. I still haven't been but know there are wild recreational options inside the mall, including a ski slope. Somewhere in the city someone is always pushing the envelope; innovations include "Miracle Gardens," "Arabian Adventure Safaris," cryptocurrency hubs, and cuisines that boast the most expensive "burger-stack" (sold for 36,700 AED/US\$9,991).[8] A documentary mentions Dubai's AgriTech farm,[9] a "cloud kitchen" that is now the sole provider for the food on Emirates Airlines. When I ask Moon where she'll stay, she says she'll find "a room"; when I ask about this room, as in how many people sleep in one room and if there's a toilet, she replies, "Sometimes four, sometimes seven or eight . . . but it's okay." Moon, like me, wants to save money. But unlike Moon, I don't have to share a room with anyone. In fact, I have a one-bedroom apartment and tell her so when she asks. I also ask if she knows anyone who could, or would want to, clean it twice a month. There's a hesitation, and then she tells me a coworker of hers has four children and is working to support them and send money back to the Philippines. It feels awkward, but I ask if I might help by offering this part-time work. Jeremy Waldron takes pains to note that cultural cosmopolitanism, as he understands it, is not about cultural "*distinctiveness*" (232) as much as the practices that unite people in their differences: "A culture just is what it is, and its practices and rituals are constitutive of it in virtue of their place in a shared way of life, not in virtue of their perceived peculiarity" (233). This "shared way of life" is worth some discussion in the context of those many, and various, who have found their way into and continue to contribute to what has become the UAE's most ambitious city. What is being shared is a level of foreignness, perhaps as true for the local resident experiencing boundary-shifting innovations as it is for itinerant workers uprooted from their country of origin to work ten- and twelve-hour shifts. Like the imported trees and quickly seeded grass that landscape so many parts of the city, we, too, are transplants in a world continually shaped and reshaped by visitors participating in an intrinsically *made* world.

⁓ • ⁓

If John Harris's town plan had ensured that residences would not exceed two stories, the influx of people across the labor spectrum created a need for multistory developments. More first- and second-class residential units pushed poorer communities farther away from development hubs. The rapid urban expansion along both sides of Dubai Creek during the 1960s also demanded a better sewage system as well as water supply networks. Ronald Griffith, an engineering consultant from the Middle East Development Division, who had been critical of Halcrow's "Harbour Scheme," was vocal about what he saw as oversight deficiencies in the town plan objectives. Issues not being addressed included building on the "flood-prone property" (Reisz 130) of reclaimed land along the creek and inadequate attention to a sewage system. Hawley, in charge of development, went ahead with John Harris's plan. Though some of Griffith's concerns were addressed, they were perhaps done too superficially; for example, septic tanks were added to the plan, but to this day, some of Dubai's state-of-the-art buildings, like the Burj Khalifa, suffer from outdated methods of waste disposal.[10]

The coordinating role of political agents the British Foreign Office now called "architects of development" (132), with Dubai's ruler Sheikh Rashid Al Maktoum, the British government, and the queen, was one of ever-changing roles and calibrations of economic variables. As development projects grew, so, too, did the profit-making margins of private consultants and businesses, many of them hired by Donald Hawley. John Harris's road plans moved developments ever farther from the port of Dubai Creek but also, increasingly, away from British oversight and control. Contractors were making their own coordinating and planning decisions with Sheikh Rashid as more land was reclaimed by the Maktoum family from the shores' edges and more concrete was transforming the desert landscape. With the British government's further distancing from decision-making power and their frequently declared position to minimally fund projects—if they funded them at all—larger and more ambitious projects were initiated by Sheikh Rashid himself.

Dubai's ruler had decided that Dubai needed its own airport. Told by the British political agent that there was already an airport in nearby Sharjah (an hour or so away by car) and "displaying the Maktoum family's healthy scepticism about British officialdom, Rashid went behind the

agent's back, secured approval from his superior the Political Resident by assuring him no British funding would
be sought, and went ahead" (Marozzi 350). Sheikh Rashid
sought financial support not from the British but from
the majlis who chose to help him. Dubai's airport opened
on September 30, 1960, "complete with the region's first
duty-free shop." As Justin Marozzi describes it in *Islamic
Empires: Fifteen Cities That Define Civilization* (2019), "In
the triangle of business, politics and religion, business
always came at the top" (350). In 1968, the British prime
minister, Harold Wilson, announced a further and consequential withdrawal of British troops from the region.
British empirical sway was waning post-World War II, as
American corporate and diplomatic clout was on the rise.
Egypt's King Farouk was deposed, and in 1956 the Anglo-
French Suez gave way to Egypt's Gamal Abdel Nasser and
his pan-Arabian supporters; Britain was losing its foothold
in what had been client states of the Arabian Peninsula.
The Trucial States were ushered into a federation; first six,
then seven sheikhdoms came together. In December 1971,
Sharjah, Ajman, Umm al Quwain, Fujairah, Abu Dhabi,
and finally Ras Al Khaimah (in 1972) joined, with Dubai,
to form the United Arab Emirates.

Interestingly, the British narrative is one in which full
support was given to this transition. Still, Dubai's current
ruler, Sheikh Mohammed bin Rashid, notes otherwise.[11]
In the Trucial States Council of the late '60s, where rulers

gathered with their delegations, the question of borders and "the border problems" remained unresolved:

> The British were the protectorate responsible for borders and maybe they could have solved the problems. Instead, they made the borders like a snake's trails. They were quite confident that this Union [the UAE] would not stand. I cannot imagine what the agenda was; if they did not discuss the border and the Union, what did they talk about? (27)

Sheikh Mohammed, in his Fortieth National Day (2011) address titled "Spirit of the Union," credits Sheikh Zayed of Abu Dhabi and Sheikh Rashid of Dubai for instigating and formalizing the union of the sheikhdoms in a meeting they had on February 18, 1968, in a tent set up in Argoub Al Sedirah at the border between the two states. There, "they sat until noon, deep in discussion," deciding on how "they were trying to ally" (33) with the other rulers. But on that day, after "they came out for their noon prayers . . . they came back for a long discussion. And I heard them . . . as I was near them, I heard Rashid say to Zayed: 'With God's blessing, you are the President,' and Zayed said: 'With God's blessing, we lay the foundation stone.'" (34).

∂ • ∂

I arrive in Dubai in August 2021, and on December 2, the UAE will celebrate fifty years since its inception. It is its

Golden Jubilee. The UAE's "Vision Statement"[12] informs us that "the Vision aims to make the United Arab Emirates Among the Best Countries in the World by the Golden Jubilee of the Union." Launched at the closing of his cabinet meeting in 2010, His Highness Sheikh Mohammed bin Rashid, Sheikh Rashid's son and prime minister of the UAE, expressed some of the UAE's foundational aspirations around "six national priorities" to be of immediate focus. It is telling that the Vision urges an always future-focused encouragement of working "harder," being "more innovative, more organized and more vigilant in examining the trends and challenges that will face us." Also, to be aware of the state of both "emerging regional and international changes," the vision toward a future of ever better ambitions is to be faced with "confidence, optimism, and determination"; imbued with what is to come, it is a tally of what has been accomplished, the foundational mortar for the possibilities of the country's future.

An illustration of the seeming paradox between how an existing reality might defy the forward-looking ambitions that built the city-state of today's Dubai is the example Todd Reisz gives of John Harris's modernizing of the Al Maktoum Hospital. Reisz begins his chapter on the hospital by noting that the fence around it was worth more than what it enclosed—an apt metaphor; he then expands to discuss how "the fence enclosed the promise of future fulfillment" (137), a sentence that could serve as the epigram for much of what was to come in the fast-developing spaces of development. That the building stood surrounded by desert, that it was "a place of last resort" in the 1950s, but that it nevertheless stood to *represent* "a legitimate place of welfare and safety" (138), is noteworthy. Given the parameters of the fenced-in space, progress could be made because it could be organized, calculated, and controlled. In 1950, when the land was first secured for the hospital, it was the merchants who provided the means to build it. When Harris first visited in 1959, there was little health care to speak of, despite the hospital's visual representation for the British agents, of "a place of welfare and safety." In 1960, Donald Hawley saw another opportunity in an improved hospital; he saw a way to earn the gratitude of residents in the provision of medical care, and that this would "more directly and more effectively than, say, harbor improvements" be a source of political leverage, and "priced much cheaper" (143) than engineering projects.

In the end, the refusal to lend money for the Al Maktoum Hospital meant the British government's views on what this would do for the local population was little more than aspirational. Tellingly, it was "an aspirational rehearsal of appearances" (145) that would then, like the funding for Halcrow's "Harbour Scheme," be shouldered by Sheikh Rashid. In his chapter on the "piecemeal" assembling of the hospital, Reisz makes the point that it was the visual evidence of such things as the "bright white bandages worn by the discharged patients" that, like the garbage collection, convinced the residents that something was being done to improve the quality of their lives. People were also being vaccinated or forced to be vaccinated when arriving at the port.[13] In short, it was the visible, demonstrable consequences of organization, the attention to what could be controlled and regulated "within the fence" that put out the messaging that Dubai was safe and hygienic—it managed, for example, to avoid a 1960 cholera outbreak that hit Pakistan and India (148).

∾ • ∾

Dubai, or modernizing Dubai, was always a blueprint ahead of itself. The aspirations, maps, town plans, harbor schemes, "a continuing improvement" and "an optical assurance" (149) made visualizations of future plans and their reality one and the same thing—at least to those who funded them. Like the airport that opened in 1960, the harbor, and now the hospital, the Al Maktoum family and the majlis provided the financing. The logistical irony was that the British agents (from Peter Tripp to Donald Hawley, and then James Craig) and development officers like James Halcrow wished to monopolize the market with British hires, from contractors and architects to engineers, people whose lack of on-site knowledge, and reliance on imported materials, or on "British [government] funding," caused delays. Given the escalating prices the merchants were now charging due to a growth in business as building materials were in demand, by 1960 the population had grown in a year by 25 percent, and a functioning hospital was needed that could serve a community that had seen increases in injuries and accidents.

Sometimes historically antagonistic, relations between the confederations of Gulf states that had become, under the British protectorate, Trucial states or sheikhdoms, still spurred development competitiveness. As with the Dubai airport (which Sheikh Rashid insisted on building despite the airport in neighboring Sharjah), the Al Maktoum Hospital would become Rashid's financial responsibility and growth initiative. When an Iraqi doctor, Abdussalam Mohamed Said, who had grown wealthy by serving petroleum-wealthy King Faisal II, decided to invest in building "a 186-bed hospital in the neighboring emirate" (155), Rashid wished for an equally large facility. Sharjah's ruler, Sheikh Saqr bin Sultan Al Qasimi, had also petitioned the British political agency for funds to build a hospital but was turned down. Unlike Dubai, however, Sheikh Saqr found other funding sources. Sheikh Rashid had lured trade from Sharjah when its port became silted up and nonfunctional and was now determined to have a hospital to match the plan put forth by Abdussalam Mohamed Said. Sharjah, like Dubai, regularly petitioned the British political agency for support for its projects. The Foreign Office had decided that Dubai was the Trucial state to invest in and where they set up headquarters, as Sheikh

Rashid provided free land along the creek to build the political agents' private living quarters.

∞ • ∞

Unlike the neighboring sheikhdoms, particularly Abu Dhabi, Qatar, and Kuwait, Dubai was not petroleum rich, at least not in comparison to the amounts discovered in the surrounding territories. Much infrastructure planning took place with the promise of further, more ambitious developments when "projected resources" would be made available with the discovery of oil. When oil was discovered in Abu Dhabi in 1958, Sheikh Rashid was hopeful, but despite on- and offshore drilling, oil in Dubai wasn't discovered until 1966, and only a quantifiable amount of it. Some fifteen kilometers (about nine miles) offshore in the Fateh field, 4 billion barrels of reserves were found, in contrast to Abu Dhabi's 92 billion barrels (Marozzi 354). The window of opportunity oil revenues would provide was finite and marked specific limits for what this financial gain could produce; diversifying the economy would have to be a priority and not be miscalculated.

As any long-term reliance on oil revenue was never an option for Dubai, the need to find other revenue sources became something of a blessing in disguise. If oil revenue did provide much of the funding for Dubai's "spectacle of development" (164)—before the climate challenge was on the table and oil was an environmental issue—it was its fast-expanding real estate projects and ambitious infra-

structure initiatives that distinguished the sheikhdom from
neighboring states. Rents from the reclaimed land of the engineered harbor made Sheikh Rashid all the more confident and
bolder in his decisions to make good on what one American
consul described as an "economic phenomenon . . . largely
based on optimism" (164). It was the vast and empty desert
around John Harris's town planning and Donald Hawley's
developments that spurred the promise, or the spectacle
of promise, that would inspire projects beyond the recon-
struction of the Al Maktoum Hospital and the reengineered
harbor. Beginning in 1969, with a large percentage of Dubai's
oil being exported by US-based Continental Oil Company,
the city was attracting investors beyond Britain; American
companies were also finding opportunities, exporting cars,
and setting up banks.

Dubai's first national bank, National Bank Dubai
(NBD), was founded in 1964. Like the Al Maktoum Hospital, it symbolized particular modernizing values in the
structural signifiers of the buildings themselves: images of
safety, security, and hygiene were evoked by the hospital's
step-by-step upgrade and technological improvements,
while a sense of orderly business transactions and markers of status, wealth, and stability were expressed in NBD's
"clear-cut lines made of metal and concrete" (168). Its
location on Dubai Creek's reclaimed land also represented
a contrast to Deira's bustling, messy waterfront, with its
wooden dhows, souks, and bartering methods for secur-

ing profit. NBD's appearance served, like the Al Maktoum Hospital, to advertise change as much as these buildings prepared to enact those changes.

The NBD building in particular represented a confluence of ways of life and livelihoods. NBD's first investors were from the region—Kuwait, Qatar, Lebanon—with some funding from Britain's Grindlays Bank,[14] making it more global than local, with stakes in "Dubai's necessary global reach and Great Britain's part in it" (167). The cultural interstices go deeper than the surfaces might suggest, the surfaces being the imago signifying "the optimism" of interleaved interests that brought a centuries-old trade economy into the twentieth and then twenty-first centuries. "The vagaries of the port" included loan transactions, gold trade, and "stateless pilgrims" looking for work. Gold should also be read in the context of Baudrillard's simulacrum, a metaphor as much as a material, signifying "the baroque of images [that] hides the grey eminence of politics." On the Dubai Creek, "where the gold trade started and ended" (168), gold, and the banks that facilitated its trade, connected Europe, South Asia, India, and beyond.

Whether gold, cash, labor, oil, or other trade artifacts, the movement of goods and people has defined, and continues to define, the cosmopolitan nature of Dubai. Being *in the world*, as Jeremy Waldron describes it, "whether he has particular affection" for the culture one finds oneself in, is the kind of cosmopolitan that moves as much between centers of trade, as spaces of displaced persons (re)locating themselves for reasons of economic and/or sheer survival. If profitable investments were being made with British imports, engineers, and developers, escalating real estate projects meant that labor, especially cheap labor, was in demand. Before the UAE's founding, it was the British political agency that "often looked the other way so as not to disturb the unrecorded flow of people needed to build Dubai," labor "in the form of illegal immigrants especially from India, Pakistan, and Iran" (169) was building the city and the city's future.

As I make my way around the city, I again notice what seems to be particular groups doing particular jobs. I know for a fact that I have been hired because of my American education and because I was affiliated with a US institution before coming to Dubai. I've often wondered if I would have had the same luck had I applied for the job from Greece, where I've lived most of my adult life. My colleague Sarah tells me, "If you go to any high-end restaurant, you'll see that the waiters are all white, usually Europeans." I smile wryly at the connotations of this: a white European serving local Arabs and their visitors to the region—after so many decades of the reverse. This, too, is a cosmopolitan moment. As was the moment I got a WhatsApp text from Yusef, a young Egyptian who pulled up as I was on my way to teach and asked if I needed a ride. He could get me to school for less than the twelve dirhams I was paying a Careem cab. I'm not sure why I got in, as I know I would not have done this in Athens or perhaps anywhere else. But I was late for work and had a sense Yusef was just looking for a way to make some extra cash, as were so many drivers, advertising their services on various Facebook and Instagram platforms. (When I say this to my pal in New Jersey, she is appalled by what she calls my "stupid naiveite"—was she right, or was she caught within the frames of her own cultural lens? It turns out this is not as rare as I assumed it was: someone on my floor tells me he does the same, that someone offered him a lift and gave him his number, which he's used since.) We exchanged WhatsApp texts after Yusef told me not to spend money calling him on my regular phone plan. Our rides went on for little over a month until the packaging company he worked for transferred him to Abu Dhabi.

∽ . ∽

The UAE's "Vision Statement" for the 2021 Golden Jubilee maps the nation's "pillars" into "six national priorities":

1. Cohesive Society and Preserved Identity
2. Safe Public and Fair Judiciary
3. Competitive Knowledge Economy
4. World-Class Health Care
5. Sustainable Environment and Infrastructure
6. First-Rate Education System

The Vision points out that these six committed priorities are part of "our responsibility towards our country" and "[aim] at empowering both the country and its citizens by reinforcing the national identity, spirit of confidence, and sense of responsibility that will build stable families and a coherent society based on authentic Islamic and Arabic values." There is more, which I'll quote later, but I want to pause on a point of interest regarding the underpinnings that work toward the Vision. The main idea is precisely that the "Vision" is a gaze into an aspirational future that sees itself "building a diversified knowledgeable economy that will be powered by the best competencies to ensure long-term prosperity for the UAE." This was certainly embraced by Sheikh Rashid bin Saeed Al Maktoum and by Sheikh Zayed bin Sultan Al Nahyan of Abu Dhabi, the two most influential sheikhs of the region, when they came together in 1968 to invite other members of the Trucial States to join the federation that became the UAE.

Given that the UAE does not, to date, have a naturalization process by which migrants and long-term contractual workers might gain citizenship, foreigners outnumber the indigenous population by as much as 90 percent.[15] In 1985, 4.4 million of the Gulf's workforce were foreigners; in 2008, it reached 10.6 million.[16] These figures are rough estimates, as exact figures are not officially available. This "*rentier* labor migration pattern" particular to the UAE and other Gulf Cooperation Council countries Saudi

Arabia, Bahrain, Kuwait, Oman, Qatar—provided a necessary workforce during the bonanza development years
of the "oil decade" (1973–1982), particularly in Saudi Arabia, Kuwait, and Oman. But in Dubai, where oil was a late
and limited arrival, it was and continues to be, a real estate,
trade, and now tourist economy that attracts and relies on
the influx of diverse pools of labor. As Dubai comprises
an Islamic majority, rather than describe the population
as majority Arab, which would exclude Iranian, Pakistani, and other Muslim populations, the question of a
"Cohesive Society and Preserved Identity" becomes complicated; a paradox in the idea of cohesion as it might be
linked to national identity is that Dubai has been shaped
by a history of trade between disparate populations who
have also served mediating roles, and been agencies, in a
shifting geopolitical landscape.

As Noor Naga notes, of the reductive "unhelpful categories" of citizen/immigrant in "Who Writes the Arabian
Gulf," there is a more tenuous, "third culture" category of
belonging regarding "what it means to be a body uncomfortable in space: to be outside looking into, or inside
looking out of the Arabian Gulf; to be invisible, or hyper-
visible; to be trapped, or forced to move continuously, like
an outlaw."[17] Meanwhile, what I notice so vividly on Fridays,
Islam's day of "congregational prayer," Ṣalāt al-Jumu'ah (the
word for Friday in Arabic is Jumu'ah), is how the many
gather inside and outside the mosque in the neighborhood

where I live. It is mostly men (there are some women as women are not obliged to join given their traditional roles in the home), and they are of all ages, carrying prayer rugs rolled under their arms or folded in their hands. Today I see a very young boy in the smallest white thobe I've yet seen, holding his father's hand, his own tiny rug in his hand. They sit on the islands in the middle of the road, outside the Carrefour supermarket, on the pavement, and in the mosque's parking lot, on their spread rugs. People I sometimes recognize as the Pakistani guard in the apartment building, the Palestinian building manager, the Talabat delivery guys, as well as Careem taxi drivers who have parked their cabs on the roadside are there. "Sister," one tells me when I think he is free, "after the prayer time, at three, I can take you." The low, persistent Aum or Ōṁ fills the air as a God is addressed in the rhythms of prayer that gather so many. The sound opens time and reminds me that a people have been here for centuries.

∾ . ∾

When in 1969 the British political agency wanted to restrict immigrants and limit the number of "non-Arabs," given the large influx of Iranian, Pakistani, and Indian economic migrants, Sheikh Rashid refused, putting out an announcement—that bypassed the political agent—in which he assured "our guests who are working in Dubai . . . [that] the government's intention is to continue its present policy which welcomes those guests whose intentions are to serve and make [an] honest living." The announcement closes with, "God bless all!"[18] It was in the interest of all parties—foreign contractors were no exception—to represent the expanding town-city as the profit-making oasis it was becoming, particularly for foreign investors. What the gold trade had done for the markets that operated through the port and creek, the real estate boom was doing for a city whose visual attractions were the consequence of new construction expanding ever farther from the creek. "Build it and they will come," Dubai's current ruler, Sheikh Mohammed, Rashid's son, said famously—and they did build, and continue to build, ever more impressive, expensive, and commercially lucrative structures.

If Halcrow's "Harbour Scheme" was a first indicator of what expanding infrastructures could do for commerce, the airport was another. It was not only a way to lure business away from Sharjah, but it made it easier to move goods. Sharjah had held the lead in the gold trade, imported from Britain and the United States, until the opening of the Dubai airport in 1960, when "its gold imports reached $20 million, nearly doubling in a year's time, providing as much as $8 million in profits" (179). Then in 1971, Rashid scratched a blueprint for a four-berth expansion of the Dubai port entrance for a sixteen-berth expansion that by 1976 proved itself still too narrow for the demand. The response was yet another, now vaster port at Jebel Ali, some twenty miles away from the creek, "carved out in its entirety and, when finished, would offer more shipping space than San Francisco." With Sheikh Rashid, Queen Elizabeth II would inaugurate the opening of the "one-and-a-quarter-mile long, sixty-six berth Jebel Ali Port" (Marozzi 353). As airports and ports were being built out of reclaimed coastlines and desert, John Harris, once again employed by Sheikh Rashid, was educating local engineers, and Rashid himself, on the practicalities, as much as the seductions, of design surfaces.

Beginning with the NBD building, "one of Dubai's first with an elevator," Harris's design established guidelines that would be incorporated into later building codes. Harris was also using glass, considered "a symbolic expression of modernity" (187), used in the airport's construction. But unlike the airport (which Harris did not design), he did not want to produce an unintended "greenhouse effect," given the high temperatures of the desert. With the electricity Kuwait and Qatar helped fund, there were now also air conditioners. Harris's design kept direct sunlight considerations in mind as much as his attention to details evoked a modern banking environment. There was "a signature stair leading to the mezzanine" and a reception area where "surfaces were cool and understated, with details left to large gestures in marble, tile, aluminum, and glass" (186); the description is telling and evocative, too, of a contrast in optics. As the real activity, or bustle, took place in the back rooms, or "back area" where, as Reisz evocatively notes, "the open banking floor [was] servicing the cosmopolitan trading elite," this is, if you will, more expressive of the souk culture, or market buzz. Here were "the babel of voices: Arabic, Urdu, Hindi, Farsi, and English when necessary." There are no "lavish marble work surfaces here, only a grid of industrial-issue metal tables at which each banker manned a typewriter . . . [and] customers were offered a wooden folding chair" (189).

Jean Baudrillard tells us that simulations are opposed to representations (rather than expressive of them), as a representation starts "from the principle that the sign and the real are equivalent," so that marble surfaces represent an equivalence with a modern banking space; whereas a simulation "envelops the whole edifice of representation," as in while everyone is negotiating in the back area of NBD in multiple languages indifferent to the optics of their environment, they are en*acting* representative methods to arrive at agreements, and in the simulation are making of their transactions a reality. The first buildings that signified Dubai's modernizing impulse were also representative: the Al Maktoum Hospital, the NBD building, and the airport with its duty-free shop, all providing the spaces, and opportunity, to enact the practices of modernity.

∾ • ∾

A quintessentially "entrepôt" state, which *Webster's* defines as "an intermediary center of trade and transshipment," Dubai, beginning with the Dubai Creek Port, was defined as such by the British agency during the decades of its presence in the region. As the town expanded beyond the port's nexus of trade, "entrepôt" could also be read as a space of cultural cosmopolitanism. The entrepôt state, defined by its role between "intermediary" spaces of trade, is a place of transactions, tenuous in its balancing act among players. If John Harris's first town plan grew from providing basic infrastructure to the port town into more representative and ambitious projects, the purpose was always to reflect a sense of permanence and security; more modern representations would communicate a quality of stability. It was this changing visuality in the desert landscape that follows what Baudrillard describes as "the successive phases of the image" as it moves from representational modalities to a fully simulated reality, one that ultimately forgets or erases any of its originating connection to the reality it may have once represented. I think of Khalid Albudoor's poem "All That We Have" as both ode and lament in the imaging that brought about Dubai's modern present.

> Because no one is there
> We will lie down
> On the shoulder of a dune
> Gazing silently
> At colors of far hills
> We wait for no one
> You might say

> No more Bedouins
> They disappeared
> All of them
> Before we knew them

The Baudrillardian stages of what happens to the image's representational power, or gradual emptying out of such, is as follows: "1. [The image] is the reflection of a basic reality. 2. It masks and perverts a basic reality. 3. It masks the absence of a basic reality. 4. It bears no relation to any reality whatever: it is its own pure simulacrum" ("Simulacra and Simulations"). Further down, the lines of Albudoor's poem tell us:

> And I would say
> Look carefully
> Behind our dune
> I can see their souls approach us
> Rising from the mirage of distance
> Or
> Appearing to us from
> The future.

Here the future has become another mirage.

❧ • ❧

If one were to translate or expand "entrepôt" to signify the liminality of Dubai's imaging of itself, one would read it as an always-intermediary space, or threshold, between worlds as much as between cosmopolitanisms; its reinventions and adaptations have moved it through Baudrillard's four stages of simulation to its present postmodern articulations. Zeina Maasri coins the term "translocal visuality" to discuss modernist transformations of Beirut in the '60s, a helpful way to speak of Dubai's visual landscape as "a force field" of changing images. She notes, "I am less concerned with the movement of a single image and object-centered approaches, than with an image's aesthetic and discursive *interrelationships* with other sets of images" (16, my emphasis). Maasri cites Deborah Poole's useful differentiation between the terms "economy" and "culture" to clarify that one group might share in the enjoyment of a certain product (economy): i.e., drinking Minute Maid orange juice, while remaining in different worlds (culture) (17), i.e., Dubai and Atlanta. I would like to read how John Harris's architectural projects helped change Dubai using Maasri's translocal visuality as a way to think about intersecting economies through their visual representations.

The NBD building served as a template signifying a base for investments and as a link to global economies, including the movement of gold coming in on flights from London and Zurich, which made its way "to the banks lining Dubai Creek."[19] If, as Reisz suggests, "the building was an empty monument to itself" (189), it was less "the reflection of a basic reality"—Baudrillard's no. 1 in the process of simulations—and more a combination of steps 2 and 3, as it both "masked" a certain perversion of that reality; that is, a bank functioning as it would anywhere else in the world, and served as a site of an economy that was culturally liminal, entrepôt rather than absent, dependent on whose gaze it appealed to, which for the time the building existed expressed a narrative of "financial optimism."[20] Unlike many after him, John Harris was attuned to the surrounding environment that was the desert climate, as much as the culture of those who would people the spaces he was building. He adjusted his consideration of the use of glass in particular. This is to say that, like his improvements and expansion of the Al Maktoum Hospital, his additions, and interventions, attempted to be in sync with the existing requirements and structures he was choreographing for particular visual effects. Reisz's discussion of how Harris went to specific lengths—creating deeper interiors, for example, to maintain a cooler temperature and avoid the overuse of glass—is indicative of a sensitivity to the environment, and context, which those who came after him often overlooked for the sake of the visual spectacle and its excesses.

The banks that came afterward were higher and more assertive in their uses of glass and aluminum as markers of modernity. "Glass—reflective, not transparent—no longer evoked concern or liability but instead the facile relationship between technological whimsy and global banking" (187). It wasn't only the banks, though they were indicative of a visual economy channeling the gaze of progress. With the discovery of oil in 1966, Sheikh Rashid was further emboldened to pursue key projects under way and add new ones. Oil was going to make the city (and not just for a few families) a place where health care, commerce, and real estate would be accessible to the many. The harbor project at Jebel Ali was in the plans when Sheikh Rashid wanted a new hospital, this one also designed by John Harris. As with the Al Maktoum Hospital, Rashid Hospital would be within a specified compound, an enclosed space defined by its health-care function. The oil-funded projects—the Jebel Ali Port, Rashid Hospital, and eventually an expanded world-class airport—expressed both regulated parameters, vastly imagined as they were, and ownership. To be outside these parameters, these markers of progress seemed to suggest, was to be outside the claims of security and purpose the developments were built to serve.

"Health City," the complex of Rashid Hospital, became a model for today's many "Free zone clusters" with their purpose-specific titles such as "Academic City," "Internet City," "Sports City," and today's "Healthcare City" (Dubai Healthcare City/DHCC), which proliferate throughout Dubai. Like Harris's 1960 plan for a municipality that mapped roads, neighborhood blocks, and garbage collecting, among its organizing characteristics, Rashid Hospital's budget was concretely and exhaustively itemized: "Each ounce of steel, hardwood, and Formica paneling was accounted for. Even a portrait of Sheikh Rashid to hang in the lobby was a line in the budget" (213). Another function, or consequence, of the concept of a compound, or "campus," was, as Reisz points out, that it could, in its concrete deliverables, be viewed "like a product, as something that was purchased, not built" (209). Reisz's insight is key as it describes what evolved. Today's "Healthcare City" or DHCC—development clusters are generally referenced by their acronyms—is "an economic free zone governed by the Dubai Healthcare City authority."[21] Like Harris's "Health City," DHCC is a domain unto itself, with on-site self-sufficient operations built as much to attract investors as to serve its patients/clients.

Among other firsts, Rashid Hospital was the first drive-in "city." As the Al Maktoum Bridge connected Deira, or old Dubai, with the spreading enclaves of inland neighborhoods and beyond, the bridge also made access to Health City possible from both sides of the creek. It opened in 1973, "one of Dubai's first major drive-to-destinations" (216), and within Health City itself were—as exists in today's micro-clusters—landscaping, streetlighting, and amenities meant to both clarify and assure. Very much the spirit of the "Oasis" that is Silicon Oasis, with its Digital Park of plasma screens advertising coming attractions that remain virtual and aspirational. The messaging of these foundational infrastructure achievements told the world that Dubai had the resources and know-how to care for them as much as it reassured local residents, both foreign and national. In the chapter devoted to Rashid Hospital, Reisz uses the words "coherent" and "legible" several times to emphasize how the hospital especially—but other structures also, such as the NBD building—were deliberate visual assertions of competency. To further emphasize how these enclaves separated themselves from the surrounding desert, and the possible "incoherence" of various other parts of the environment, there was to be grass, "mature plants," and fountains;[22] this upgrade of visual and verdant landscaping meant to signal more comfortable and attractive spaces also asserted its difference from the less cultivated surrounding environs, which was, for the most part, desert.

As with the landscaping of Health City, Harris's original town plan had islands and gardens in its neighborhood units or "blocks"; it was a way, in Reisz's words, to "stitch" the disparate parts of the city together. What, of old, were desert oases of stopping points, now were human-made islands of imported green. This confluence of the made and indigenous, the constructed and adapted, would constitute an ongoing dialogue between desired aesthetics, their appeal, and the demands and facts of the desert climate. It's of interest that as Harris's projects proliferated and became more extensive, the attention to such things as "solar positioning and the use of reflective light to minimize interior temperatures" gave way to more focus on "air-conditioned interiority" (220), which defined modern, urban living. It also emphasized that life could be lived along the standards of cooler, northern countries despite the desert climate, that this, too, could be worked around. The Dubai airport (opened in 1960), Rashid Hospital (opened in 1970), and Port Rashid (fully functional in 1972) were there to foreground specific functions. They were also, to borrow Zeina Maasri's words, "politically situate[d] image-makers" that "demand[ed] recognition in disparate circuits of competing visuality" (19). The desert, and what remained "outside" these constructed (now air-conditioned) environments built to serve, and signify, the standards of a modernizing city would, by contrast, suggest a kind of blank—a still-to-be-transformed potential of space—rather than the desert reality in and of itself.

What, then, to return to Maasri's point regarding "circuits of competing visuality," is left out of this selective lens on a fast-expanding city? Certainly, the discovery of oil in 1966 gave Sheikh Rashid more leverage in his decision-making (and borrowing) capacity; while he was generally aligned with the political agents and invested in British engineering expertise and technology, he made his own decisions. If the lens on a developing Dubai of the late '60s and early '70s was preferential to British or Western aesthetic choices, such as John Harris's solid functionality and use of British templates for his designs, there were exceptions. A hospital donated by an Iranian medical aid organization that exists to this day was dismissed by Julian

Bullard, the political agent at the time. Apparently, unlike the plainness of Rashid Hospital, it had lavish additions of "mosaic-bearing facades, marbled entranceways, and vinyl wallpaper"; yet what seems to have irked Bullard the most, beyond what he read as aesthetic extravagance, was that all of it, including "the flowers" and "the earth" (227), came from Iran. That the medical equipment was "of the highest quality"[23] didn't seem to play any role in how the hospital was assessed—and ignored—in British and American brochures advertising the city and its opportunities. Something else that remained invisible in this lens was the increasing number of laborers coming from India, Pakistan, and South Asia.

It is useful to use Maasri's term "translocal visuality" to discuss the selectivity of how Dubai's growth opportunities were read by the different constituents involved in its developing narrative. Maasri notes, with Jacques Rancière, that there is a "dividing up" that is "at once political and aesthetic" regarding "visuality [that] embodies an experience of judgement of taste that has the potential of segregating the space of the social" (41). While Dubai's growth moved it away from the Dubai Creek, newcomers who were connected with banks, oil, and engineering companies, whose numbers grew, were becoming wealthy and also populating the new "swaths of desert" that "kept the rich separated from the poor" (233). This was another beginning. The term "free zone" would proliferate, as areas that elicited trade and business, like the port, catered to those who wished to make good of an "openness to all"[24] policy, if policy is what one can call Rashid's laissez-faire attitude toward the promise of profit. Here, too, John Harris was commissioned to draw up a new town plan that would accommodate how "Dubai's landscape responded harmoniously to new oil wealth" (236), and here, too, the messaging was to present a city's clear, stable, development along the lines of the town plan he had made in 1960; there would again be enclaves of self-sufficient districts, Jumeirahs (residential coastal developments), with their ring roads, cinemas, parks, and marinas.

Bounded spaces steer the gaze toward what takes place within them, putting what exists outside of "the fence" at a literal remove; it maps how to identify, and hence control, what takes place within those parameters. While John Harris's ambition was to further connections between the proliferating districts of the city's oil-enhanced economy, building roads to link Dubai's various spaces—particularly the Deira part of the city and the new rapidly changing landscape—Harris's control or "master plan" was hard to maintain. What Reisz calls the "legibility" of the city, which up through the '60s, and until the British quite suddenly declared their withdrawal from the Middle East, was very much the creation of Harris's and Halcrow's engineering and architectural projects. With the formation of the UAE in 1971, the Trucial sheikdoms came under one flag, and the two most powerful cities—now states—Abu Dhabi and Dubai, led the way, with Sheikh Zayed of Abu Dhabi becoming the UAE's first president. "Legibility" would now shift from the control of British influences, political and otherwise, to a more openly entrepôt trade ethos of converging methods and cultures. While the British and others had made good use of the city's cosmopolitan approach to trade—read as transactions over different economies—the movement of gold being one and of oil being another—the UAE's formation, and Dubai's continued growth, put that cosmopolitanism within other frames of legibility.

Ever focused on keeping Dubai a trade hub, Sheikh Rashid did what he'd always done: he assessed and negotiated, in consultation with the majlis, and then acted. With oil exports providing the needed income, Rashid aimed to maintain what the British had started: to make Dubai a "model" for other Trucial States. This time, however, the city-state would model a global city. With the discovery of oil, Sheikh Rashid envisioned a "petroleum state" and looked to cater to those contributing to the ambition—namely, but not solely, British and American corporations such as the Continental Oil Company. As with the case of Dubai's first infrastructure projects, the visual change was a material expression—it signified a hoped-for reality as much as it did a present, if still-to-be-developed, potential. To recall Albudoor, "Because no one is there / We will

lie down / On the shoulder of a dune / Gazing silently /";
in Baudrillard's step 2 of an image's simulacrum, it "masks
and perverts a basic reality." Rather than a masking, the
buildings that focused attention were enacting a "translocal visuality"; in the spirit of Maasri's definition, such
visualities expressed a "movement of particular ideas" and
"aesthetic practices" of image making (18). They expressed
hybrid influences on a changing visual landscape that simulated a reality still to exist.

Dubai's Clock Tower was one example of the desired
image of a petroleum-rich city being projected to the world.
It suggests both Baudrillard's interpretation of a "perversion" as much as it was a translocal model; it was "Dubai's
monument to oil"—a "four-meter-high steel abstraction . . .
'buff pink,' something reminiscent of two Moorish arches
intersecting at ninety-degree angles" (Reisz 240). Another
example of what might be called "intersectional," which
demonstrates something of both the perverse and translocal, is a film commissioned by BP meant to narrate how
oil profits were building a modern city: *Dubai*[25] (1970)
was made to demonstrate a city "on the go," with its British director Rodney Giesler using images of "rush hour"
traffic, water taxis, and people busy with phones to suggest
a cosmopolitan frenzy; it was another montage of projections. It also conflated history, as Reisz points out, with
what came before the discovery of oil and the "new Dubai"
of improved amenities, such as clean water, electricity, and

modern housing, that left behind a past where "residents relied on ingenuity to survive." The twenty-five-minute film does not so much "mask" as it erases the city's colonial past, with examples of "the British agency's role in first hampering Dubai's trade growth and then later pushing its urban development" (241). As such, to return to Baudrillard's steps in the process of simulating realities, what is rendered as reality, through a history of Dubai's adaptability to circumstances often beyond its control—such as the devastation of their pearl-trading economy in the 1930s—goes from what "masks and perverts a basic reality," to Baudrillard's step 4, the masking of "the absence of a basic reality." In Giesler's *Dubai*, the British are all but peripheral to a focus on the majlis, Sheikh Rashid's entrepreneurship, and most importantly what the discovery of oil made possible.

Dubai and *These Are the Trucial States* are films that craft narratives of the future: What will a future, not yet arrived at, be shaped by given the geographical and entrepreneurial conditions and their confluences of opportunity? What happens, these films seem to ask, when climate and geography—but also advantage, as in the trade of pearls, gold, and then oil—converge with the engineering and managerial expertise of the West? Certainly, in these films, it is a Western gaze on a blank desert that "peoples" the space of the city and fills that blank (from a Western lens) with a future: *Dubai* "celebrates more of what does not exist: 'taxes and form-filling' and 'red tape'" (242).

But also, the absence, and need for, a Westernizing infrastructure that is now made more possible given the economic advantage of oil—at least this is the messaging. In what Maasri calls "the entanglement of global cultural flows," she suggests that a "globally pervasive 'society of the spectacle'" (18) is generated. And I consider how that came to define what began with the economic advantages the discovery of oil provided. A previously environmentally inhospitable space, these films seem to say, is made less antagonistic thanks to the influences of foreign investments, aid, the ingenuity of the indigenous population, and the boldness of its ruler, Sheikh Rashid Al Maktoum.

With the formation of the UAE, British political influence and administrative control could no longer "fence in" Dubai's growth—to borrow Reisz's metaphor for the measurable parameters of John Harris's renovations of the Al Maktoum Hospital. Harris continued to work on increasingly ambitious projects financed by Sheikh Rashid, including a new town plan, one that asked engineers "to slow down when they were under the chronic pressure to speed up" (251). Yet he, like other developers and engineers, was caught in a wave that figuratively, and literally, blurred earlier markers of what had been seen as coherent "units" of residence or work areas marked off, or "fenced off," for specific purposes. Roads were extending the reach of the city's boundaries, as they now created access by car to once isolated pockets of development. Harris encouraged the building of more "development rings," a practicality as much as an aesthetic intervention to help control sometimes congested roads, and different peripheries of development, while keeping ever-larger "concentric circles around the old harbor" (255). If Harris's 1971 town plan was in tune with the expanding city, it still harked back to Dubai Creek as the central trade hub, with the Al Maktoum Bridge leading to the city's farther reaches.

❧ • ❧

The 1971 town plan shared a thematic continuation with the 1960 plan to make Dubai "legible" in practical as much as aesthetic terms, with an efficient infrastructure at its functional heart. But the ambitions of the 1971 plan would not pan out according to Harris's vision; perhaps it was already too late to reign in what was well under way: something not manageable within the terms of legibility Harris had laid out for a city that was, in 1960, still a port town around a creek. Nevertheless, the "marina-themed residences" and "artificial islands" would become one of the many features of what was to become "new" Dubai. Reisz tells of a contradiction between Harris's "written" plan and his "illustrative" one—the illustrative being the one that "outlines the undeniable direction of Dubai's sprawl," while the written plan tried to contain it, keeping the city "centered" around the creek and its historical heart. Tellingly, Reisz notes that "instead of demonstrating how a creek-centered city might grow, the illustrative plan drew the eye toward the new city's blank spaces," a city whose reaches, or "designations" would be accessible by the newly asphalted roads. It was where there was blankness that Sheikh Rashid envisioned the future, as "blankness signaled boundlessness" (258).

"Blankness," or desert space read as potential, does not so much "mask" the "absence of a basic reality," to use Baudrillard's template, as much as it simulates the reality of a potential. John Harris's illustrative map of roadways and "development rings" led away from what already existed, the known that Harris wished to build around, that would give way to the unknown via the "organizational spine" (268) and the main artery of road travel that was Sheikh Zayed Road. If Harris represented a British "legibility" to Dubai's infrastructure, a postcolonial or post-British influence involved a more translocal confluence of developers like Khalaf Al Habtoor. Al Habtoor had already been involved with projects such as the Rashid Hospital before he commissioned Harris to build the Metropolitan Hotel—the self-sufficient "neighborhood units" of the '60s had given way to enterprises that now catered to the singular vision of individual developers and their clientele.

One might assume that the convergences of enterprise and expanding communities would, by extension, enhance convergences of cosmopolitan fluidities. But while the influx was there and growing with an estimated population of 100,000[26] in 1971 (which was likely higher), the influx, like those bounded areas catering to particular needs, remained stratified with Dubai's poorest migrants situated in "planned districts" (255) outside of the city's broadening parameters. How a translocal agency of visualities might be navigated once John Harris's "written plan" was overwritten by the spatial blankness of his "illustrative plan" becomes a question, too, of how a particular visual cosmopolitanism grew to reflect a population in varying roles. Maasri writes of the "diverse and highly fluid fields of visuality" that was Beirut in the '60s, as "a force-field entangled in relations of power" where the hegemony of particular visualities obstructed the diversification of such fluidities (20). More simply, constructions like Khalaf Al Habtoor's Metropolitan Hotel, the proliferation of banks,[27] the widening (again by Halcrow) of the Al Maktoum Bridge, and, most arrestingly, Dubai's World Trade Center, expressed very specific hierarchies—particular groups were being catered to, and served, in developments and buildings that existed in specified areas for a specified purpose.

Not just the "districts" but the visual appearance of developments, inclusive of the roundabouts, fountains, green spaces, and cinemas, told a story of class and status, belonging, and not belonging, or not-quite-belonging, and how Dubai was serving, and shaping, those stories. Despite the economic boon the discovery and export of oil provided, Dubai was not Abu Dhabi, with its plentiful reserves. Dubai, instead, would promote and build itself to be the most service-oriented, comfortable, and techno-logically cutting-edge state of the UAE. It would also build the region's first skyscraper, the Dubai World Trade Center (DWTC), a clear marker and message to the region and the world that the city was a beacon of progress. Commis-sioned by Sheikh Rashid and designed by John Harris, the skyscraper was "a showpiece," a signifier of the "new Dubai," and a space, like the city that was meant to be, emblematic of a new era. The World Trade Center had "dedicated exhi-bition facilities" that included offices, convention centers, entertainment facilities, a hotel, and luxury apartments. Like other developments, the thirty-nine-story building received criticism for being too ambitious, unrealistic, and impractical (it was far from the city and hard to get to). Yet like those projects such as the Jebel Ali Port, it came to prove Sheikh Rashid's foresight in the ways the construc-tion would symbolize, and make good on, the vision of a city that would lead in the global markets it catered to.

A large swath of land "in the middle of nowhere," near the border with Abu Dhabi, was allocated for the World Trade Center, a name that unabashedly replicates the World Trade Center (WTC) under construction in New York City during the same period; in fact, Harris's first sketches of the building had twin towers like those in Manhattan. Rather than a translocal visuality, the DWTC represented an overt reproduction of a building emblematic of Western first-world trade; it was less representative of any "reflection of a basic reality" (Baudrillard again) than a desired projection: here, "an idealized community would come to life, pressed into the tower's stacking of 1,225-square meter-floor plates" (287). As this complex was pitched for its corporate-deal-making spaces and high-class amenities, John Harris—again aware that this was being built in the desert and not, for example, New York City—begged the question of how optics might conform to a projection. The desert was read concretely—in terms of climate and temperature—and metaphorically—in representations of spatiality and its suggestions of potential. To recall Maasri's reference to Deborah Poole's distinctions between economic and cultural visualities,[28] Maasri writes of Poole, "I take her distinction as a cue for considering transnational circuits of modernism as conduits of visual economies rather than shared visual cultures" (19). The DWTC represented a visual economy rather than a visual culture; its resemblance to New York City's WTC marked a shared ambition that included becoming a major center for commerce—a tab on the DWTC site reads: "From beacon of possibility to global business hub"—although the cultural contexts of the two buildings couldn't be more disparate.

One clear marker of difference was environment: the use of glass in the desert would intensify heat, and John Harris was reluctant to use it. Despite being one of the optics of modernity, Harris, in earlier projects, had been sensitive to how architecture and building materials might enhance or offset the heat. Gordon Heald, Harris's chief designer, created "a well-shaded interior" that provided a "modular façade . . . [that] split the building into two layers" and which remains, according to Reisz, "one of Dubai's most remarkable towers, though its double-façade has unfortunately only scarcely been replicated." It was fabricated in situ using British aluminum and glass but was nevertheless a "translation of a traditional Arabic arch" in its assemblage.[29] Something of a footnote, but indicative of Deborah Poole's valuable differentiation regarding cultural and visual economies, is a remark cited by Reisz in quotes, attributed to Harris in his reflections on his career in the Gulf. Apparently, the space between the two facades constructed to offset direct heat was "enough 'for a very thin man' to clean windows and perform maintenance" (288). To frame this statement in the context of Maasri's discussion of visual politics and radical cosmopolitanism, it's important to understand the role of capital as an organizing catalyst within the economy of Dubai's visual transformation.

What transnational fluidities made possible another "site of bounded control and isolation," and what was the narrative that enhanced and appropriated aspects of translocal cosmopolitanism that had less to do with a shared visual culture than it did with a visual economy of shared purpose? The narrative, as Reisz documents it, insisted on a building made to the standards of any expert construction in the UK, that abided by requisite standards and took into consideration the environment, as in the fact that the concrete was sulfate-resistant so as not to be eroded by subterranean chemicals in the desert swamp.[30] the storyline followed a template that catered to British standards; like New York City's WTC, the DWTC was as much an expression of a visual culture of shared environment as it was of a visual economy that conflated the two buildings. As Reisz describes it, within its bounded context, isolated from the rest of Dubai's commercial hub, which in the '70s would have still been around Dubai Creek, the DWTC's site was a "re-imagining . . . as if it were on British land," and the "contractor's public statements made it seem, for example, that the hundreds of workers manning the on-site casting stations for the tower's concrete parts were British" (292). The reality was that the hundreds, then thousands, of construction workers who operated the stations, and those who built the complex, lived in barracks and on-site tents and were for the most part from South Asia.

∾ · ∾

How is a narrative reconfigured? What shifts in the gaze when what is left out or erased materializes in the "blanks" or "blank spaces" of, say, John Harris's mapping? Let's suggest that "the vast territory" in the 1971 master plan that was read as a space "of even more opportunity" (289), peopled with transplants, most of whom, in that narrative, are British, was articulated more factually: "The South Asian workers, sometimes described as Bernard Sunley staff [Bernard

Sunley & Sons being a British property development company], were deleted from the construction narrative in order to project a truly British-built undertaking. In this way, their labor was calculated into the companies' logistical computations, handled similarly to daily temperature forecasts and shipping schedules and housed on site with other construction supplies" (294). The unseen, elided, human labor collapsed into "logistical computations" ignores the non-British contributions that were essential to the major construction projects of the evolving "new Dubai." It also evades, or more precisely "perverts," in Baudrillard's rendering, the reality of a visual culture; Pakistani workers' expertise, for example was left unmentioned; the visual simulation—a World Trade Center in New York City[31] — was meant to suggest that the DWTC was as close to being a Western construction as the WTC itself.

Which vision scripted the "new Dubai" would depend on whose gaze was scripting it. As the DWTC was being built, Sheikh Rashid would take his guests to view the city from the height of its highest storied level—the levels increased as the building developed—insisting it be the tallest building in the region; it would eventually reach thirty-nine floors. Sheikh Rashid kept amending an initially eight-storied building; the "bounded site" of the project extended to align with an always-further (or higher) ambition. As Reisz details John Harris's attention to projects' operating and maintenance demands in the desert climate, the visual economy and optics of progress were continually being adjusted to the newest requirements. DWTC grew in additions and apartments—495 apartments were added, inclusive of washing machines and cutlery—and services from car rentals, a post office, cinema, and "limitless parking" (300).[32] Inside the bounded (and air-conditioned) interiors with their carefully planned functions, the requirements for trade, and those involved in it, were provided for; anything from their originating cultures would be part of this economy too.

Outside the complex of DWTC, and other fast-growing developments whose interiors boasted shopping malls, ice rinks (the Galadari Galleria had a permanent ice rink), and cinemas, was the apparent messiness of old Dubai, where things like fire hydrants and garbage collection were still rare or missing. Outside the carefully manufactured, and manicured, gardens and compounds with their amenities was another visual economy and culture. Deepak Unnikrishnan's 2017 novel, *Temporary People,* is a fantastical rendering of, among other things, the ambitiously choreographed sites comprising the UAE's main cities of Dubai and Abu Dhabi. His linked vignettes recount the surreal trials of those thousands who, like the soulless materiality of glass, steel, and concrete, have themselves become material. Unnikrishnan's "Chabter Seven," "In Mussafah Grew People," is a parody of the region's growth narrative. Told from the perspective of "a little sultanate ruled by an envious little grump, Sultan Mo-Mo," whose "royal blood boiled" at yet another Western anchor's praise of "Dubai's vision" (47); Mo-Mo, "peeing green" from envy, is told that he, like Dubai, can grow labor. A "Malayalee scientist . . . had been helping the al-Nahiyan and the al Maktoum families grow Malayalees on secret farms cocooned inside industrial-size greenhouses in Musaffah, around forty-five minutes away from Abu Dhabi's city center." The "Canned Malayalee Project" comes about when the labor minister needs to "multiply its workforce by a factor of four if the sheikhs were to accomplish the growth they envisioned" (49). The fiction's wild, often darkly hilarious rewriting of the positivist narrative of progress shows the carefully bounded sites, constructed by initially British developers and engineers, to be factories of disposable and exploited labor too.

Unnikrishnan's novel, which won the Hindu Prize in 2017 and the inaugural Restless Books Prize for New Immigrant Writing, is prominently displayed in Kinokuniya, Dubai's largest bookstore, located in the Dubai Mall. In "Spectral Sovereignty, Vernacular Cosmopolitans, and Cosmopolitan Memories," Homi K. Bhabha cites the different cosmopolitanisms that arise when people who have not chosen to be together nevertheless find themselves in close proximity sharing lives: "In Dubai that is one of the issues of South Asian migrant workers. They literally live closer together than they would ever live otherwise" (143), an example he uses to suggest that the discussion of cosmopolitanism(s) should begin with what is not foregrounded in mainstream narratives of cosmopolitan agency; it is precisely this lens that Unnikrishnan's work amplifies as he exposes as illusionary those totalizing narratives of belonging. Noor Naga notes that stories like Unnikrishnan's "complicate our notions of transience and belonging, of victimhood and oppression, of race and class. And in doing so, they are paving the road for new narratives of ownership by non-citizens" ("Who Writes the Arabian Gulf" *The Common*, 25 Oct. 2021).

III.

I am in a car with a Pakistani driver, Rana, who tells me he has been to Dubai for stints of two to three years, for what is coming up to a cumulative six, but he doesn't want to stay anymore. "How can I stay? No one here can become a citizen. You cannot say, this is *my* home!" He's right,[33] though people stay for lifetimes, and some do call it home. In its most recent incarnation, under Sheikh Mohammad bin Rashid Al Maktoum, the city is a tourist and entrepreneurial mecca with alluring theme parks and a plethora of commercial-free zones. "Arabian Adventures"[34] has its own sign at Customs for anyone entering the country through the government-sponsored Emirates Group. It is sometimes hard to know, or see, the difference between what is meant to be an entertainment venue and what is a business venture, two areas often linked. It is also a cultural inheritance; during the building of the DWTC, "Sheikh Rashid's advisors stressed to Harris 'the importance of amenity and recreation . . . in the interest of trade'" (Reisz 299). The many iconic photographs taken by Ramesh Shukla that document the region's pre-federation years, as well as its more contemporary moments—those of Sheikh Zayed and Sheikh Rashid together in conversation, signing documents, and with various dignitaries are among the most moving, as the two are often drinking tea or coffee with a tray of it in a metal teapot (Al dallah) nearby. Venues for entertainment or what would now be termed "Wellness" were, at Sheikh Rashid's request, to be a part of the large developments John Harris was commissioned to build; luxury hotels, apartments, and shopping malls were included in the DWTC complex of exhibition halls and conference spaces.

"Critical cosmopolitanism," a term Walter D. Mignolo uses to discuss the consequences of globalization on cosmopolitan movements in emerging/colonial modernities, interrogates "coloniality as the constitutive side of modernity" (722). What built progressively ambitious infrastructure projects that came to fulfill a visual narrative of modernity in Dubai also expressed makers of globalization. Todd Reisz notes that when it came time to inaugurate Dubai's World Trade Center, where at least "fifty British companies" (307) were involved, Queen Elizabeth II was visiting the region. It was 1979, and the British had withdrawn their political presence in 1971 with the formation of the UAE; nevertheless, the British monarch, visiting the Gulf peninsula on February 26, 1979, cut the ribbon of the DWTC with a pair of gold scissors handed to her by John Harris. In Reisz's words, "Dubai's government maximized her thirty hours in the city to emphasize the city's British-sourced modernization," a launch that messaged the DWTC as an example of "British achievements" (309). Even though the DWTC, and major projects such as the Jebel Ali Port, were financed by Sheikh Rashid, the optics of "permanence and stability" as markers of progress and competence were still conflated with the face of British empirical power (to this day, electrical outlets take the British three-pronged plugs). Positioned at the beginning of the twelve-lane Sheikh Zayed Road, the DWTC expressed a possibility even more than a fact: Dubai was moving ever farther from its beginnings on the creek, and trade was as much a language of transactions as it was a gamble for the city-state's future.

∾ . ∾

The French anthropologist Marc Augé's seminal work on non-places articulates the liminalities of spaces where locality—an intimacy with the specificities of place and its connections to identity—are upended. His work helps to contextualize some of the speed and consequences of Dubai's evolution into what Augé writes of supermodernity;

it is Baudrillard's definition of "the desert of the real" where empires of old are replaced with simulations and technologies that function "with the same imperialism [that] tries to make the real, all the real, coincide with their simulation models" ("Simulacra and Simulation"). If old Dubai, with its crowded streets, souks, earthen and coral-built houses with their wind towers (*barajeel* in Arabic), and majlis, represented the locality of the creek, new Dubai follows a gaze that leads ever farther from such markers. What signified progress—for example, air-conditioning as opposed to wind towers—signified specific representations of modernity. The old districts of Deira, like Bastakiya, were being reconfigured in the mid-1980s, a result of a commission Harris's firm competed for; Sheikh Rashid's home, or palace court, would be renovated while maintaining Islamic architectural features such as arches and wind towers. The ruler's diwan (court) would take up a large part of the Bastakiya district where, Reisz notes, the confluence of aesthetics, the "fanciful contrivances attempted a new history, not because there was no history but because a real history was not preferred." Historically a "mix of cultures and time periods"[35] (328), Bastakiya's houses were being demolished for newer constructions, and its residents were being asked to leave for districts where they were given plots of land or apartments.

While an aesthetics of modernity (inclusive of British manufacturing materials) shaped the transformative infrastructure projects developed and engineered by John

Harris and William Halcrow, after the formation of the UAE, more overt features of Islamic art were being used to construct an imagined history. Arabic signifiers that included "wind towers, falcons, dhows, the sinuous curves of dunes and camels" were "signaling a fictive ancient city" (330) as the glass and steel high-rises continued to etch the outlines of "new Dubai." If the "fenced in" or "bounded" sites of projects such as Rashid Hospital delineated the possibilities, and parameters, of progress, with its clear "checklist" of needs and attention to purpose, the newer formulations regarding design criteria, as demonstrated by the ruler's diwan, was to present yet another narrative by which to read the city; perhaps as a counternarrative to that of coloniality, it traded in its own fabrications. If the inspiration had less to do with what British political agents and developers like John Harris saw as Dubai's possibilities and legibility, the "new Dubai" enacted a confluence of imaginaries, a more overt invitation to a multiplicity of projections.

By the mid-1970s, John Harris's town plans and maps had given way to a script of a fast-expanding territory with expanding projects. Harris's plans were no longer legible within the frames he had used to organize, and legitimize, a once-struggling port town as it grew into a city. If Harris's first mappings expressed an "operational" connection to the spaces it organized, projects like the DWTC enveloped as much of "an imaginary" of fabricated "hyperspaces" (Baudrillard) that simulated realities—like the wind towers of the ruler's diwan. Todd Reisz concludes his exhaustive work on how architecture made Dubai with an invitation to regard the city's ongoing narrative as yet another act in the performance of its modernity; the stage has changed, and they are now many: the "territory" following Baudrillard has as much to do with the spectacle of the city's various incarnations as it has to do with who is doing the imagining. I will suddenly realize on one of my visits to Downtown Dubai, where the Burj Khalifa stands surrounded by a fabricated lake with its spectacular fountain shows, that it no longer looks to me like a syringe with its fine needle pointing into the sky but rather a modern-day minaret with its thinning, silver spire gleaming above the rest of the city's skyscrapers.

∞ · ∞

I pass various building clusters on my way back to the flat after having been away for some months. There are many new islands of green, and they are, like me, and Rana, who is driving, transplants. Multiple date palms have appeared seemingly overnight, and their trunks are decorated with strings of tiny lights as if to say this too is decoration—yet another way to make an otherwise empty stretch of space into something inviting. As we drive, and Rana tells me more about his decision to leave and join his brother in Italy, where his Albanian wife has a sister that she would like to introduce him to, an occasional automated voice interrupts with a repeated "You are speeding. . ." when

Rana slips over the ninety-kilometer-per-hour limit. Interspersed reminders along the roadside, with their happy or unhappy emojis reading your speed, tell you how you're doing. I think of these moments as something of an inheritance from the "fenced-in" spaces of old, such as that of the Al Maktoum Hospital compound, where the fence marked a boundary between an ordered compound and the unmapped vistas outside of it. Any boundary is a signifier of what its border is meant to protect. There is an inherent paradox at the heart of a city whose ongoing ambitions keep pushing the borders of what simultaneously contains it. If British political agents helped ensure Dubai's survival after its pearl trading economy collapsed, its inherently intersectional cosmopolitanism has also been key to the city's evolution.

In a region where some 90 percent of the population are transplants—visa-carrying guests, and/or foreign investors—the UAE, but Dubai especially, has branded itself as the region's innovator, always ahead of the curve and amenable to the latest market demands. A callback to the days of the city's first development projects, when more basic needs spurred infrastructure. Today, the DWTC site advertises itself as a space where "185 countries are represented" with "3M+" visitors annually" and "50K countries exhibiting"—its free zone space is a constantly adapting platform ready to accommodate entrepreneurial start-ups to trade in digital assets. In the leaps and bounds the city, and now nation-state, has taken to achieve its global presence, an intuitive sense of timing, with the courage (not a few have called foolhardy) to risk, has been a recurring generational theme of the Al Maktoum rulers. When in 1984 Abu Dhabi's Gulf Air was refused preferential landing rights at the Dubai Airport, it dramatically reduced its weekly flights "from eighty-four to thirty-nine." Instead of buckling under the pressure to give in to Gulf Air's demands, Sheikh Rashid borrowed US$10 million, leased Boeing 737s from Pakistan, and in 1985 launched Emirates Airlines, now one of the Middle East's largest carriers, having overtaken Gulf Air (Marozzi 350).

How does a boundary maintain its border-ensuring role as it simultaneously invites inclusion? In framing a space, attention is directed to what is being framed. If people like John Harris and Donald Hawley, the political agent, provided some of the first frames by which to read a developing town, it was the gaze into a future that those first maps, or framings, later made possible that would overwrite them. As Todd Reisz has noted, it was also the blank spaces beyond the municipal development plans that inspired the Al Maktoum rulers' ambitions (260–262). Dubai's World Trade Center, for example, was both "the materialization of Dubai's economic freedom," and "a site of bounded control and isolation." And while Harris had been contracted for the construction, it was not part of his "predetermined land-use zone in a master plan. Rather it was a piece carved out of the 1971 development plan's white blankness" (289).

Among the six key elements, or pillars, articulated in the UAE 2021 "Vision Statement" for the country's fifty-year Golden Jubilee is "Cohesive and Preserved Identity," another framing. As Rana pointed out, only a UAE national can entirely belong, as citizenship is not extended to anyone not of the region by blood or lineage. It is another marker, yet it does not preclude what began more than ninety years ago with the British outposts in the Gulf: the visitor/outsider is here to contribute, make a profit, and eventually leave. But like much else in the region, accommodations for the foreigner's stay can also be exceptional. Today one might buy property in "freehold"[36] zones, or areas where some of the most sought-after real estate exists, to own, rent, and resell for up to ninety-nine years.

⁀ . ⁀

In his articulation of a "critical cosmopolitanism," Walter Mignolo suggests we look at modernity from the critical perspective of what has, in fact, *built* it, beginning by deconstructing a Western narrative of "a civilizing global design" (722) that glosses the links of coloniality to modernity. Rather than eliding the underpinnings of what he calls the "global designs" of such "civilizing missions" as the spread of Christianity or Marxism's project of emancipation, Mignolo proposes we be attentive to "the borderland seen from the perspective of those 'to be included'" (724). In the context of Dubai's urban growth—an achievement as visually as it is operationally spectacular—the exteriority or "borderland" can be read as both the borderlines around the city's various project mappings and those spaces apart from them, such as the camps where most of the laborers who built the projects live. Mignolo, distinguishing between those "cosmopolitan projects" that define modernity as consequences of the larger narrative of coloniality, argues a need for articulations of what is located in spaces that modernity's gaze has not conflated: "By *exteriority* I do not mean something lying untouched beyond capitalism and modernity, but the outside that is needed by the inside" (724). In other words, the interdependencies of the ways capital is accumulated have often been kept invisible, or misarticulated, in the story of modernity and its exploitations.

When I read Mignolo, I think again of Unnikrishnan's *Temporary People* and lines such as: "'What will you do with all this wealth?' a beaming sultan asked the three men. 'Purchase bling from Gold Souk. Then leave. Start a business back home, stay indoors, wipe the sun off my face' grinned Pinto, his knees rattling" (53). I hear versions, or rather riffs on the theme, in the time I've been here. There's Susan from New Jersey, who has been in the region for eleven years and tells me she is ever grateful to the UAE. She's not wealthy, but she's managed to carve out a decent living, save money, and help put her nephew through college. If she had stayed in the United States, she would be adjuncting and most likely have to do so at more than one institution to cover basic expenses. I meet various expats at various gatherings, but it's the men I see on the patches of green who illustrate Mignolo's point of "the outside that is needed by the inside" most acutely. The slender men who drive the Careem and Talabat food delivery motorbikes, with their square metal boxes, are taking a break. The bikes are parked sometimes haphazardly next to patches of green where the men, sometimes in groups, stretch out on the grass. I have never seen a white driver, and they always look like they're enjoying the reprieve, lying on the grass checking cell phones, dozing or sitting cross-legged on the manicured islands of green between the road and compounds of villas I pass when I walk to my apartment after a teaching day.

As Bruce Robbins and Paulo Lemos Horta have noted, "cosmopolitanisms"[37] is a word that "would look naked without its final 's'" (10). We need our Emirates I.D.s to open a bank account, and we are here temporarily. But we are also part of a majority who don't belong by any connection of nationality or citizenship, though our lives and interactions make for "a sort of cosmopolitanism by default, aimed more at the everyday cohabitations and negotiations of diverse groups than at the conceptual goal of transcending cultural differences and producing a universal concept of humanity" (14). Perhaps Dubai has stumbled upon this fact unintentionally in the very compartmentalizing of how labor and its clusterings have been organized; the "oases" and "cities" represent outposts of shared purpose, as much as solitudes.

EXPO2020, hosted in Dubai, was built on a stretch of land off the Sheikh Mohammed Bin Zayed Road between Dubai and Abu Dhabi. Yet another "bounded" site, it covered some 45 thousand square kilometers (17,375 square miles), an area larger than Monaco. This was in 2019, and because of the Covid-19 pandemic, the exhibit opened on October 1, 2021. I visited several times and now wish I had gone more often. At the exhibit, 238 participating countries created 193 pavilions organized according to theme rather than continent—itself a cosmopolitan rendering. Shared ambitions were the vectors rather than the geopolitical markers of economy or geography. As John Harris had done, allotted spaces for the different pavilions and events were named districts and grouped according to three themes: Sustainability, Opportunity, and Mobility. To walk through the wide, cleanly paved spaces and discover what countries had chosen which district was an education in how aspirational goals for a sustainable future were being choreographed by individual nation-states. Ukraine, for example, like the pavilions of the UAE, Saudi Arabia, South Africa, Vietnam, the United States, and Somalia, was among the countries in the Opportunity district. Sweden, Cambodia, Turkey, Yemen, Georgia, Qatar, and Germany were among those in the Sustainability district, while Mobility included Togo, Russia, Albania, Iran, Oman, Finland, Mexico, and Poland.

EXPO buses shuttled visitors free of charge from different parts of the city; UAE residents over sixty were granted free passes. The exhibits were often spectacular, foregrounding a country's strengths as much as its future hopes, from ways to capture rainwater to irrigate areas of drought in Mexico, to the simulated fog and snow of the Swiss Alps, to ways a Finnish company recycled plastic bottles into T-shirts. Of the forty or so exhibits I managed to see, I counted Italy and the UAE among my favorites; the smaller pavilions (which did not so much represent smaller countries, as smaller economies) included Cambodia, Oman, Uzbekistan, and Mozambique. Many had restaurants or cafés serving the country's culinary highlights. There were teas and sweets from Uzbekistan and the incredible scent of frankincense in the Omani pavilion, where smoking frankincense and plasma screens transported you into a world both contemporary and ancient. You could buy frankincense, labdanum and myrrh, incense and oils, face and body creams, as well as perfumes. I wish I'd bought some of the frankincense that was on sale: it is expensive because it's rare and comes from the Boswellia Sacra tree that grows in arid deserts found mainly in Oman, Yemen, and Somalia. The Boswellia was the pavilion's main recurring image: from a large center-piece with hanging crystals meant to suggest the sap of frankincense to videos of it in the Omani desert that told the story of the sultanate's history.

EXPO2020's theme of "Connecting Minds, Creating the Future" speaks to the ongoing vision of the UAE project as it foregrounds innovation and growth. On my ticket for the pavilion is the logo "Land of Dreamers Who Do"; the space itself, as one enters the premises around the pavilion—a remarkable white-winged structure built to suggest the spreading of a falcon's wings (the UAE's national bird) by the Swiss-Spanish architect Santiago Calatrava—is spectacularly modern. And yet, with its surrounding stream and what look like potted mangroves in their midst, plentiful birds, and wide spaces to sit on jute carpets, the nation's premodern beginnings are also evoked. Inside the pavilion, one is taken on a virtual tour of animated scenes from the region's history. Images of Sheikh Zayed bin Sultan Al Nahyan of Abu Dhabi, the UAE's founding father and first president, animate actual mounds of sand meant to simulate a journey through the desert. Guests walk through and between these dunes where lines like "Welcome to the Desert of Dreams" in Arabic and English and "Rooted in our humble beginnings, a resilience that continues to this day" are projected onto the sand as is the story of the UAE told with black-and-white stills of the past. I was deeply moved by the story as much as its presentation. The dim lighting and

voice-over, with its interludes of ambient oud music, trans-
port us through iconic moments in the nation's formation.
Newsreel clips where Queen Elizabeth II is speaking with
Sheikh Rashid, or Sheikh Zayed pulls up in a black Mercedes
next to a dune, then walks the desert sands in sandals and
his flowing *ghutrah* (headdress) to consult with others as
they gaze over the desertscape, take us on a virtual journey.

Marc Augé's invaluable *Non-Places: An Introduction
to Supermodernity* (1992) has given us the language to
discuss the differences between what he defines as "non-
places" and "anthropological places" where identities are
rooted and histories embedded in relational as much as
transactional economies of exchange. "Non-places," on
the other hand, foreground transience and temporality;
they are spaces rather than places, though such distinctions can overlap; that is, you can be in the space of an
exhibit located in a particular place. Spaces (rather than
places) do not provide a continuum of history in their
more ephemeral, abstract iterations of location. Augé cites
supermarket chains, hotels, airports, refugee camps, and
exhibit halls as examples of non-places. The EXPO pavilions exemplified non-places as sites of virtual realities
where the traveler-visitor constitutes as much of the site as
the spectacle itself: "we should still remember that there
are spaces in which the individual feels himself to be a
spectator without paying much attention to the spectacle.
As if the position of the spectator were the essence of the

spectacle" (70). After the EXPO2020 exhibition closed, a taxi driver I met from Pakistan told me how much he loved it, that it still made him happy, weeks after it was over, to think about "all the countries" that were "like a cinema"; he hoped "they keep open forever."

Augé suggests of the spectator-position that "the landscape he is contemplating or rushing through" is a positionality that invites the subject to project, and name, what becomes part of the experience of a non-place; also a space in which Baudrillard's "hyperreal" supplants a physical reality with what the gaze on it produces:

> Space, as frequentation of places rather than *a* place, stems in effect from a double movement: the traveller's movement, of course, but also a parallel movement of the landscapes which he catches only in partial glimpses, a series of "snapshots" piled hurriedly into his memory and, literally, recomposed in the account he gives of them, the sequencing of slides in the commentary he *imposes*. (Augé 69–70, my emphasis)

In the landscapes of the hyperreal, the spectator, positioned in the fiction of his own projection, manages to simulate experiences of "anthropological place"; in other words, the cultures of countries on exhibit in the EXPO pavilions became singular journeys for each visitor.

EXPO2020 showcased the potentials of the future as much as the pavilions were sites of cultural landmarks and events. In the Ukrainian pavilion, for example, the signifiers for the country—video footage of sun-kissed fields of wheat—made for a hyperreal moment given the subsequent fact of Russia's invasion and what now has transformed those fields into zones where tanks, soldiers, and corpses are the reality. The non-place of the pavilion itself was also reconfigured by the spectators passing through it; in the entranceway of the exhibit, Ukraine's president Volodymyr Zelenskyy (pre-invasion) speaks optimistically to a virtual audience through a plasma screen, listing the country's achievements, particularly in the realms of digital technology. Dressed in a suit and tie as he smiles and addresses his imagined listener, the image is startling, given the fact of war and what the current world has come to know of the handsome leader in battle fatigues updating the world on the dire realities of his country's tragedy, his concentrated look and furrowed brow now iconic. Augé describes a "melancholy pleasure" derived from the solitude experienced by travelers who feel "an overburdening or emptying of individuality, [in the presence of] the movement of the fleeting images" (81). There was certainly no dearth of visitors in the Ukraine pavilion and indeed a sense of melancholy given the circumstances; there were also the traces we left as we passed through. The pavilion's walls were covered in handwritten Post-its from visitors from around the world wishing the people of Ukraine all the courage, love, and support they deserved. The condition of melancholy

Augé speaks of, connected as it is to a detachment from any relation to "anthropological place" as a condition of supermodernity, gives rise to "a very particular and modern form of solitude" (86), a cosmopolitan solitude that is the recognition of our ephemeral condition, nowhere more tangible than in war zones and spaces of transience.

Not surprisingly, Augé references Walter Benjamin's *The Arcades Project* (1927–1940) in his discussion of supermodernity. His word choice is striking: "We know that Benjamin's interest in Parisian 'passages' and, more generally, in iron and glass architecture, stems partly from the fact that he sees these things as embodying a wish to prefigure the architecture of the next century, *as a dream of anticipation*" (86, my emphasis). That the story of Dubai's modernity is an embodiment of Benjamin's "dream of anticipation" is uncanny. Dubai's contemporary landscape suggests one shape Benjamin's "architecture of the next century" has taken, and the Al Maktoum rulers have demonstrated how concretely this anticipation was realized. The slogan "Build It and They Will Come" frames this anticipation: "they" are a group that is not "us" but one we need, and wish, to invite in. It is the basis for a cosmopolitanism in which "the other" coexists with the subject. Yet the terms of this coexistence are as specific as the development clusters that map the region. Certain groups need visas, and anyone who lives and works in the UAE needs a Residency Permit. But within these parameters is, as the saying goes, a world, or many of them. As Robbins and Lemos Horta note in their introduction to *Cosmopolitanisms* (2017), "The old cosmopolitanism was a normative deal. Less an ideal than a description. The new cosmopolitanism merely assumes that wherever and whenever history has set peoples in transnational motion, sometimes very forcibly, it is to be expected that many of them and their descendants will show signs of hybrid identity and interestingly divided loyalty" (9).

The traveler as cosmopolitan figure in more classical ideas of cosmopolitanism becomes more broadly liminal when framed within the context of supermodernity. Or in the context of what Bruce Robbins calls a "redistributive cosmopolitanism" (49), the traveler is also of those classically left out of the discussions of cosmopolitanism; those enjoying the high-end amenities of the Burj Al Arab Hotel (completed in 1994) are not Talabat and Careem motorcycle drivers taking a break on the islands of grass in front of villas. Yet both are "on tour," so to speak, within the spaces they inhabit. Both are part of the 85–90 percent of nonlocals living in the UAE. While your Talabat or Careem driver would be an unlikely guest of the Burj Al Arab, they might very well have visited the EXPO exhibit, and if they were over sixty, they could have visited for free for as many times as they might have wanted to. This is not to undermine obvious inequities but rather to refocus them within the broader context of urban capitalist economies and the nation-state. Robbins's "redistributive cosmopolitanism," or what is now referred to as a "cosmopolitanism from below," aims to "redistribute" the lens on the cosmopolitan subject who finds themself in different geographical or cultural locations out of necessity as much as choice, whether it is the French chef in the kitchen cooking for elite clientele in the Burj Khalifa or the South Asian worker on a construction site working ten- to twelve-hour shifts. As Justin Marozzi points out, "Sheikh Mohammed claims his inspiration for Dubai is tenth-century Cordoba, which may be less fanciful than such a comparison initially appears. The Andalusian capital was open, trade-friendly and cosmopolitan, a ferment of literary expression and [a] laboratory of intellectual discovery" (359).

Of the installations in the UAE EXPO pavilion, I found especially moving a globe of thin metal about two to three meters (about 6.5 to 10 feet) high that stood in a dimly lit corner against an image of the sea and rolling sand dunes; the color's silver-blue glint made the sea look like it was washed in moonlight. The globe was open, ornamental, with various shining artifacts hanging from it that suggested the different objects of trade exchanged over the centuries. A voice-over narrates the stories of those who have traveled these pathways over sea and sand, continents and cultures. Written over the dunes and serving as a lit path are the words, "A journey of objects, ideas, beliefs and techniques . . . as a crossroad for millennium, we continue to open our minds and our homes to the world." Text and image become catalysts for imagined worlds, what Jean Baudrillard argues has led to "the desert of the real," but what becomes, too, a space of potential, of the sometimes-tenuous interfaces of the virtual and material. "The Desert of Dreams" is one of the slogans in the UAE pavilion, signifying (without Baudrillardian irony) dreams born of the desert. A real desert where the gaze, or gazes, on it have changed its face, from Sheikh Rashid's ever bold ambitions to the entrepreneurial initiatives of Sheikh Mohammed that earned him the name "the CEO Sheikh." What looks back at the observer has as much to do with how the observer interacts with what they see. "It is always a question of proving the real by the imaginary," writes Baudrillard, which gives the imaginary a signifying priority that can bring on a "pure simulacrum." Khalid Albudoor's poem imagines a lost Bedouin culture that will appear from a future that appears as a mirage. What Baudrillard sees as "the desert of the real" has created venues that make up Dubai's cosmopolitanism spaces. There is, for example, a purely simulated "Global Village" off the Sheikh Zayed Road where so many "cities" and "villages" veer off that central, organizing highway.

Global Village, like Baudrillard's example of Disneyland, is another hyperreal experience of simulations, though unlike Disneyland, it also provides markers of what Augé calls "anthropological place[s]." In some ways, it is a model of the tensions that describe Dubai's cultural hybridities. Caricature-like edifices of different countries' iconic structures, such as India's Taj Mahal or Greece's Doric columns, are grouped next to each other as if they were parts of a Hollywood set; one enters these "sets" only to be introduced to the very real wares of different countries. Initially taken aback by the inelegant artifice of it all, I was quickly immersed in the tastes and scents of what I was experiencing. A large, very large, ring of high wood counters took up most of the space for Yemen, around which vats of honey were on display. As we passed, men in their dishdashas urged us to taste the honey in their amber golds, blonds, and dark browns. The variety included honey laced with ginger, others with turmeric; some were a thick, motionless sap, others spilled like juice. Afghanistan had hand-woven and fruit-dyed rugs that exuded a raw wool scent; there was clothing on sale and an abundance of lapis and much silver jewelry. Africa was loud with music. Women from the stalls wanted me to try the African Shea butter, offering to rub the backs of my hands with it. The bustle was that of a crowded but organized market suffused with the smell of baking potatoes, smoking corn, grilled sausages, and the sweet coconut scent of sticky rice and mangoes. The later it became, the more people arrived with the cooler temperatures. Outdoor venues like Global Village are open from October through March, when temperatures fall from highs of 103–99°F to lows of 88–80°F, though rarely below 73–70°F. As we make our way around

the stalls, I'm reminded of a remark attributed to Paul Gilroy by Asad Haider that any diasporic gathering of people
enacting the cultures they carry or embody disrupts hege-
monic ideas of "cultural nationalism"[38] (111). Despite the
kitsch of the artifice that makes no attempt to suggest it is
otherwise, the bustle taking place was a reminder that the
market culture of old Dubai's souks continues here, too, in
this "bounded" space of simulated countries.

∽ • ∽

What aspects of place engender or enhance a sense of
belonging within locations of difference, or non-places
that are ever-changing? What makes for any "common
ground" when such does not formally exist? If one belongs
by citizenship or nationality, this is a moot point. In "The
Cosmopolitan Experience and Its Uses," Thomas Bender
describes the contemporary or "new" cosmopolitan subject as someone whose experience is "consequential" to
them, and "moderately unsettling" (121). Perhaps in the
non-places of our multiple transient venues, the common
ground is as much a projection, virtual or otherwise, of
shared interests as it is a product of our individual solitudes. As visitors to Dubai, we are "in contractual relations
with it (or with the powers that govern it)" (Augé 82);
that is, an Emirates Residency card will give you an entry
point into multiple platforms, including the ability to
open a bank account with NBD. But entry points, like any
bounded cluster, make for their own "shifts of gaze and

plays of imagery" (Augé 75); the visitor is made legible within frames outside of which, like the desert blankness, they remain unspecified. The existentialist anxiety of what these parameters suggest of our solitudes is cosmopolitan—it roots singular and variously broad experiences in the paradoxical fact of a distance from any common (anthropological) ground. Dubai's Museum of the Future is perhaps the city's most arresting expression of this idea of cosmopolitanism, a virtual polis of solitudes.

The Museum of the Future is stunning. Developed by Killa Design architects and engineered by the Bruno Happold consultancy (it opened to the public in 2021), the facade is made of stainless steel and consists of 1,024 pieces "manufactured by a specialist robot assisted process; covering a total surface area of 17,600 square meters"[39] at a height of 77 meters (225 feet). A crescent-shaped circle covered in the calligraphy of Arabic quotes from His Highnesses Sheikh Rashid and Sheikh Mohammed, the quotes also serve as windows, perhaps a suggestion of the city's interleaving gaze between its supermodern present and its ancient Arabic past. The grounds and the foyer of the building are spacious. But once one begins the museum visit—a bit of a non sequitur, as there are no artifacts on display, unless one counts the present as we know it to have become an artifact—one feels claustrophobic; at least I did. The online logo of the museum reads "Where the Future Lives," and just below a tab invites us to "Preview your experience." From the airy spaciousness of the entranceway, one is ushered into the closed space of an elevator where an automated voice tells us we are going to be sped some fifty years into the future, to 2071.

I had no idea what to expect when I visited with my daughter, who was visiting me. She was less anxious and more curious than I was. As we stood with others in a clearly marked space and were told to enter a large elevator, we found ourselves part of an interactive show, a plasma showing of our space-capsule/elevator looking down on images of earth. We were quickly taken to the museum's highest level and "on arrival" ushered through rooms, floor by floor; rather than any individual wanderings to observe artifacts, as the word "museum" would suggest; it is the space itself that is on display, both virtually and physically, as much as our interactive roles within it. Like Augé's passengers, we are led through controlled and specifically delineated rooms that have specified functions. We "WITNESS THE WONDERS OF NATURE" or "EXPLORE A LIBRARY OF LIFE" in a solitude that gathers us from our many points of origin: "The passenger through non-places retrieves his identity only at Customs, at the tollbooth, at the check-out counter," or at the museum, where "neither singular identity nor relations [connect us]; only solitude and similitude" (83).

Perhaps the discomfort came from a sense that the spaces the museum rendered so impeccably would indeed become the future of our lives, a pure simulation in which any originating reality would be unrecognizable, absent under "a radical law of equivalence and exchange" (Baudrillard). We would live by what Augé names "a rhetorical [as opposed to geographical] territory" (87). Among the exhibits were installations of some of the jobs that would be available in this imagined future, such as "Luna Robo Driving Instructor" in the "Applicant Pioneer" category; there was a "Hope Recruitment Center" and "The HEAL Institute," where a sign under "The Laboratory" explains: "HEAL's ecosystem simulator, where we test how new species will impact their environments." The low lighting and cool temperatures reminiscent of a laboratory showcased "specimens" from animals to plants and trees and sea life in fluorescent-colored vials and test tubes. The space, as my daughter put it, is "trippy," a kind of psychedelic journey of the mind and senses. In other text/image displays, like an interactive space for meditation and job-résumé making, we are provided with more "rhetorical territory," told in the WELLBEING room that: "Despite our technological abundance, depression, anxiety, loneliness, and addiction remain common. In 2030, depression passed obesity as the world's greatest health risk. Too little has changed in the 40 years since." There's also this in the meditation room: "A SALVE FOR YOUR SENSES & SPIRIT: Our senses bond us as humans. Sight, hearing, taste, smell, and touch are the original human technologies and keys to living a healthy, balanced life." The rhetoric is "unsettling," to use Bender's word, "an invasion of space by text" (80), to use Augé's. Where had history dropped the referential ball (to echo Baudrillard)? I resisted the idea that "smell and touch" were ever "human technologies." In the Museum of the Future, it felt as if the always forward-looking city had reached its supermodern moment of "the pure simulacrum" (Baudrillard).

∾ • ∾

Any desire begins with a projection, and Dubai, perhaps more than any contemporary city, was built, and continues to be built, to accommodate projections, from the tourist planning an "Arabian Adventure" to Ripa, who tells me she is on a two-year contract at the salon where she cuts my hair, saving to buy a home in Armenia. The built sites of what the gaze on the desert has produced are nothing short of spectacular, but they beg the question of what the costs have been, beginning with the city's carbon footprint to the inequities of labor. Yet like the Al Maktoum acumen, and audacity, that imagined and built the city-state, now a site of superlatives—the tallest building, the largest airport, the biggest mall—there is currently an initiative to make Dubai the city with "the smallest" ecological footprint by 2050;[40] it is yet another gaze into a future as seemingly improbable and incongruous with the present as was Sheikh Rashid's decision to build Dubai's first airport, create the DWTC, or keep widening the Dubai Creek harbor. "The cosmopolitan mixes unfamiliarity with recognition. The cosmopolitan is always slightly uncomfortable, even at home" (123), notes Thomas Bender, and it occurs to me that the description applies, in some capacity, to the 10 percent of Emirates that make up Dubai as much as it might describe the 90 percent of nonnative foreigners, 71 percent of which are Asian. Cultural cosmopolitanism, as Bender argues, is "*active*; it can't be reduced to a thing [or an idea]" (my emphasis), as such there is "no universal commensurability" (121), but a shared space of un-settled feeling.

A stroll over the well-shined granite floors of the Dubai Mall will dramatize some of the incarnations of newness and its radical juxtapositions. Women in full burqas, as well as those scantily clad, will walk side by side. I find myself self-conscious (and trying not to stare) when a group of very attractive and very tall young blond women in tight vinyl pants and cropped tops that looked like lingerie walked along the aisle of shop windows in statuesque confidence. The equally handsome guys with them occupied with their cell phones seemed almost oblivious as the group sauntered by. I kept wondering what the women clothed in their abayas and burqas were thinking. What the men used to their abaya-clothed women were thinking. What did I think; it confused me. I am not a Muslim woman in an abaya, of which there were many, covered in a variety of materials from black chiffon, georgette, and beaded silks to plainer cloths.

Some were intricately decorated with subtle designs along the sleeves and hems, some beautifully embroidered; the footwear was often striking and shone beneath the hems; Lucite heels, plastic or semiprecious gems, colorful straps, usually decorated manicured, nail-polished feet. Some of the contrasts gave me that "moderately unsettling" experience Bender describes. It was another "'both/and'" characteristic of Dubai's cosmopolitanism that overrides the "'either/or' structure of nationalism"[41] (141). What did I feel, too, when my student Zaina, who had come into my office to ask some questions, asked if I was "for diversity." She phrased it as a rhetorical question, as in, "You're for diversity, aren't you?" My answer surprised me as much as it did her. "Yes," I said, "but it makes me stressed." Zaina reacted with something like, "Really? Wow," and came back another time for more conversation, as I think we were both too stunned by my answer to say much more at the time.

What did I mean; it had been hard to pronounce some of my students' Arabic, Indian, African, and Persian names, and I was very conscious of that fact, especially since I knew I was not doing a good job of it. We were also masked because of the ongoing Covid-19 measures—talk about an equalizer—but I wanted very much to be sure that my English was clear and clearly heard (despite my mask) by the second-language users in my classroom. When Zaina was back in my office another day and brought up my remark, I said the idea of my difference, and inability to speak in a way that might be understood clearly enough, made me stressed. I would not be as self-conscious in a classroom where my students were primarily English speakers. There was always a moment when I read the roster at the beginning of class and asked if I had pronounced a name correctly when there was a pause as a student helped me correct my mispronunciation. I expressed this to a colleague in Sharjah who said, "Well can they pronounce your name?" An awareness, even a self-conscious awareness, of the limits of my ability to bridge difference is what has created an appreciation for what I can in fact bridge, starting with my self-consciousness. It was the topic of an ongoing conversation with Zaina. Maybe, too, this was a moment in which we were sharing, in our different contexts, a sense of our cosmopolitan solitudes. In more theoretical terms, it was a moment of what Walter Mignolo discusses as a "yielding toward diversity in which everyone participates instead of 'being participated'" (744); our differences were dialogical and critical and somehow underwrote any universalizing idea of who belonged where, and who needed to be more attuned to their sense of awkwardness. We were both feeling like "the other."

IV.

A trading post of old positioned on the Arabian Gulf, Dubai has always understood the importance of transactions, the commerce that comes of it, and the visitor who makes it possible—there is something implicitly cosmopolitan in any formulation that admits to a need for the other; how that need has changed, been channeled, and shape-shifted over time is part of why Dubai continues to invite us into a gaze we, too, help construct. "Only in the future was Dubai made to last" (317) writes Todd Reisz regarding the city's expansionary growth and aspirational resilience; a future always open to its next opportunity, one the city will script with others.

∽ • ∽

More than a year into my stay, I look out from the balcony of my apartment, and the desert is as evocative as ever. The sudden high-rises that seem to grow like date palms at its edges are reminders of the project (of construction) that is Dubai. What is the nature of this city, born of the desert, and its continued allure? I think it has become uncannily representative of a global moment, a cosmopolitanism of services in which we are both participant and spectator. We observe and greet one another from our particular enclave, or "cluster," observing each other and interacting to the extent that we trade in a shared purpose, but beyond that is the figurative, and literal, desert. "Present-day simulators," Baudrillard tells us, "try to make the real, all the real, coincide with their simulation models." Nowhere was this made more explicit than in the experience of Dubai's Museum of the Future, where "a liquidation of all referentials" disappears any equivalence with what the signs—images of plant life, oases, waterfalls—might signify. It is a space, rather than a place (to recall Augé) of simulations; a space where we, the spectators, are given the stage to author our hyperreal narratives of imagined worlds.

"When the real is no longer what it used to be, nostalgia assumes its full meaning," writes Baudrillard. I think again of Khalid Albudoor's poem. The speaker in the last section, which I did not quote in the epigraph, addresses the future, saying, "I extend my hand / Toward you / Carrying a few daydreams / This / Is all that remains for us." He returns to the region's Bedouin past as he speaks of building a tent where he will wait and "hand them buckets / Filled with water / And they, from their time worn bags, / Will hand us / Love / So we can learn it / Again" (352). Nothing is visible during the sandstorms of shamal winds that usually occur in spring and the heated summer months. Sand-filled currents of air sweep across the desert, and the city's skyline is enveloped in a reddish-yellow cloud. From my balcony at the Mirage Residences, where I am living temporarily,

I imagine what the Bedouin culture must have endured, but also, in the distance, I see a burning horizon where the vague outlines of high-rises suggest a city that looks barely real.

Photo courtesy of the author.

ACKNOWLEDGMENTS

Thank you, Kateri Kramer, for your most generous suggestion that I write this essay, and to Sam Scinta for including me in Fulcrum Publishing's Speaker's Corner series. Without a community of shared ideas, I could not have completed this project—thank you for the recommended readings, Neni Panourgia, John Dayton, Dimitra Vladimirou, Maria Daskalakis, Christina Kkona, Korina Gougouli, and Kateri Kramer; the texts were invaluable. Michel Pharand, editor extraordinaire, and first reader of the finished draft, warm thanks for smoothing out rough spots. Sam Scinta and Alison Auch, thank you for feedback that made this a much clearer essay; and special gratitude to Alison for her careful edits. Living and working in Dubai has been a lesson, among many, in navigating unknowns—a cosmopolitanism of unknowns, if you will, very much the reality of those seeking work and vocational opportunities as of those on pleasurable excursions into adventure. A shared meal or the offer of a ride was sometimes all it took to help navigate those unknowns—thank you so much for the solidarity, Yahya, Kevser, Hariclea, Pam, and, of course, Lizzie, in the language of our shared topos, *Shukran jazilan* شكراً جزيلاً

GLOSSARY

Ajman. Capital of the emirate of Ajman; fifth-largest city in the UAE after Dubai.

Al Maktoum Bridge. Separated by the Dubai Creek, connects "old Dubai," or Deira, and Dubai proper.

Arab National Liberation Front (ANLF). Saudi opposition movement founded in Cairo in 1962 and based in exile.

aum (or ōṁ). Voiced syllable with Sanskrit roots, sacred in the chants and incantations of faiths; the sound represents an invocation of the divine.

baladiya. Arabic for "municipality."

barajeel. Arabian wind tower, introduced in the 1900s as a passive cooling device that "caught" the breeze, directing it downward and cooling interiors by as much as 20°C.

Bastakiya or Al Bastakiya. A district of old Dubai, named after the Iranian town of Bastak, now the reconstructed Al Fahidi Historical Neighborhood; dates back to the 1890s.

British political agency. From 1820 until the British withdrawal in 1971, agents of the British government, then UK, represented British political and trade interests in the Arabian Gulf.

British Protectorate state (also known as "client states").
Following the treaty of 1820 that culminated in the Perpetual Maritime Truce (1853), Arab rulers' decision-making was contingent on British government approval; in exchange Britain promised protection of the territories.

Bur. "Land" or "countryside" in Arabic, the word has come to mean "area" or "district."

Burj Khalifa. Landmark building in downtown Dubai and currently the world's tallest at 2,717 feet (828 m); opened in 2010.

burqa (or burka). Outer body covering (usually black) worn by Islamic women; covers the body from head to foot, with a mesh around the eyes for visibility.

Careem. Internet platform based in Dubai that serves more than 100 cities in the Middle East; provides everything from cabs, cars, and bikes to food and pharmaceutical deliveries.

Deira. "Old Dubai" situated next to the Dubai Creek, dates back to the 1700s when it began to develop along with the creek that facilitated commerce and trade routes.

dirham or AED. UAE's official currency.

dishdasha (also known as a *kandoura* or *thawb*). Long robe or tunic (usually white) worn by Arabic men in the Gulf region; nuances of style suggest particular regions.

diwan. Designation of a powerful government official or governmental body; also, the Crown Prince's Court in Dubai.

Downtown Dubai. The city's tourist hub; home to the Burj Khalifa, the Dubai Fountain, and Dubai Mall.

Dubai Clock Tower (also the Deira Clocktower). Located at the roundabout in Deira that provides access to the Al Maktoum Bridge.

Dubai Creek, the creek. Tidal inlet that extends nine miles (fourteen km) inward and forms a natural port conducive for trade routes; historically divided the city between Deira and Bur Dubai.

Dubai International Financial Center (DIFC). Hub for tech start-ups and business entrepreneurs.

Dubai Mall. Part of the $20 billion Downtown Dubai complex; currently the second-largest mall in the world, with a floor area of 502,000 square meters (5,400,000 sq. feet).

Dubai World Trade Center (DWTC). Also known as Sheikh Rashid Tower, a thirty-eight-story skyscraper built between 1973 and 1979; events and exhibition space and business hub.

Emirates I.D. UAE Identity Card and mandatory for all residents and citizens; the only identity document (besides a passport) accepted by government agencies in the UAE.

Emirates Residency card. Permanent residency in the UAE exists only for citizens; visas for all others can be (regularly) renewed for specific periods of time.

entrepôt. Port city or town where transshipments of merchandise take place; where goods are traded, stored, reexported.

EXPO2020. Hosted in Dubai at the Dubai Exhibition Center and open from October 1, 2021, to March 31, 2022.

ghutrah. Traditional headdress for Emirati men.

Global Village. Advertising itself as a "world without borders," a compound off Sheikh Zayed road comprising ninety pavilions representing ninety countries.

Golden Jubilee. UAE's Golden Jubilee celebrated its fiftieth anniversary of nationhood on December 2, 2021.

"Harbour scheme." William Halcrow & Partners' 1955 proposal for expanding the Dubai Creek port involved deepening and widening its entrance; the British Foreign Office approved it but would not fund it; Sheikh Rashid paid for it by becoming a debtor.

"Health City," i.e., today's Dubai Health Care City. Complex that began with Rashid Hospital (1973), a public hospital built by John Harris.

hyperreal. Term coined by Jean Baudrillard; explains conditions in which consciousness cannot distinguish between reality and simulations of reality. In advanced technological socicties, the hyperreal (i.e., digitally formulated, virtual worlds) becomes part of the real.

Jebel Ali Port. Deep port located in Jebel Ali, constructed to supplement Rashid Port (the Dubai Creek harbor port); opened in 1979. The largest human-made port in the Middle East.

Jumeirah. Said to reference hot coal or burning to suggest the burning sand; refers to the beauty of coastal (now residential) areas near the Gulf Sea.

Kinokuniya. Large, Japan-based bookstore located in the Dubai Mall.

*majlis/***majlis.** Arabic for "sitting room"; used to refer to a gathering of common interest groups in Islamic countries, which can include legislative assemblies.

Museum of the Future. Impressive crescent-shaped building that is one of the latest additions to Dubai's stunning array of architectural landmarks; opened in 2021.

National Bank Dubai (NBD). Dubai's first national bank formed by Sheikh Rashid and opened on June 19, 1963; merged with Emirates Bank on March 6, 2007, to form today's Emirates NBD.

non-place. Term used by French anthropologist Marc Augé; refers to places such as hotels, airports, exhibition halls, and shopping malls where individuals remain anonymous.

"Old Dubai" or Deira. Includes the renovated Al Fahidi Historical Neighborhood, which offers an old town feel of the fishing port of old; various well-known souks are located in Deira.

Ōṁ. *See* "Aum."

Ras Al Khaimah. The last to join the federation on February 10, 1972, to become one of the seven states that form the UAE.

Rashid Hospital. Opened in 1973; part of the Dubai Health Authority and Dubai's second-oldest hospital.

Salāt al-Jumuʻah. Jumuʻah means "Friday" in Arabic, the day of the congregational prayer in Islam.

shamal. Northwesterly wind blowing over Iraq and the Gulf states that results in sandstorms; most frequent in the summer months.

Sharjah. Third most populated Emirate state after Dubai and Abu Dhabi.

sheikhdom. Geographical area (often referred to as a kingdom), and/or society ruled by a tribal leader/king ("sheikh" in Arabic).

simulacrum/simulacra. Imitation or representation of a person or object (means "a semblance of"); Jean Baudrillard argued that it is not a representation of a reality but a reality in its own right.

souk. Arabic for "market" or "marketplace"; also, an outdoor stall or bazaar.

supermodernity. Term used by Marc Augé; refers to qualities associated with late modernity, such as the overabundance of events, stimulus, information, the acceleration of history, and loss of historical memory.

Talabat. Online food delivery service founded in Kuwait in 2004 and now prevalent in the Middle East.

The Dubai Frame, or "The Frame." Described as an "observatory museum," the world's largest existing frame; opened January 1, 2018. It apocryphally signifies the gaze of the UAE's founders as they gazed toward a "new Dubai" with "old Dubai" (Deira) at their back.

thobe **(or** *thawb*)**, also known as the** *dishdasha***.** *See* "dishdasha."

translocal visuality. Coined by Zeina Maasri; discusses how intersecting economies can express themselves in their visual representations.

Trucial States. Also the "Trucial Coast" and the "Trucial Sheikhdoms," a name the British government gave tribal confederations along the coast of southern Arabia; the sheikhdoms signed agreements (or "truces") with Britain between 1820 and 1892 to ensure their protection.

"UAE Vision Statement," the Vision. Statement articulating the UAE's ongoing national agenda as it celebrated its fifty-year Golden Jubilee of union (https://www.vision2021.ae/en).

Umm Al Quwain. Located on the peninsula of Khor Al Bidiyah with Sharjah as the nearest major city southwest of it, and Ras Al Khaimah to the northeast.

United Arab Emirates (UAE). On the eastern end of the Arabian Peninsula, the country shares borders with Oman and Saudi Arabia; the seven emirates, each ruled by their own emir, or sheikh, are Abu Dhabi (the capital), Dubai, Ajman, Sharjah, Fujairah, Ras Al Khaimah, and Umm Al Quwain. Formed December 2, 1971; the emir of Abu Dhabi serves as president, and the ruler of Dubai is vice president.

"Vision Statement," the Vision. *See* "UAE Vision Statement."

Zabeel Park. Urban, public park in Dubai located in the Zabeel district; home of the Dubai Frame.

NOTES

1 See Bhabha, *The Location* 1–2.
2 See https://web.stanford.edu/class/history34q/readings/ Baudrillard/Baudrillard_Simulacra.html; all subsequent citations of "Simulacra and Simulations" are from this source.
3 See https://sps-automation-middle-east.ae.messefrankfurt. com/dubai/en/facts-figures/uae-vision.html.
4 "entrepôt. n." OED online (Sept. 2019).
5 Peter Tripp was a British political agent (Foreign Office official) to the Trucial States from 1955 to 1958; Dubai was the town where British agents began development projects to help organize these states and terrain of some 80,000 square kilometers (30,888 sq. miles) of swampland, estuaries, and desert plains.
6 The sand and water crescent from the tip of Qatar to Oman was a trade route to the East for the British Empire and home to Arab tribal chieftains. It was known as the "Pirate coast," as pirates found shelter along the rocky coastline for their fleets and menaced merchantmen passing between Mesopotamia and India. A signing in 1820 between six Arab chieftains and the British officers turned the pirate coast into the "Trucial States."
7 The Arab National Liberation Front, part of the Union of the Peoples of the Arabian Peninsula founded by Saudi dissident Nasser Al Saeed, called for a referendum on the role of the British monarchy, constitutional democratic reforms, land reforms, and nonalignment in international affairs and oil agreements.
8 See https://dubaiofw.com/most-expensive-burger/.
9 See https://tracxn.com/explore/AgriTech-Startups-in-Dubai.

10 See https://www.dailystar.co.uk/news/world-news/dubais-burj-khalifa-doesnt-sewage-26095095.

11 See Al Maktoum, *Spirit of* 26–35.

12 See https://www.vision2021.ae/en/uae-vision and https://sps-automation-middle-east.ae.messefrankfurt.com/dubai/en/facts-figures/uae-vision.html.

13 See "Al Makhtum [sic] Hospital, Dubai, Annual Report & Returns 1960" (19 Jan. 1961), National Archives United Kingdom (NA) PO371:157067.

14 See Davidson, *Dubai: The Vulnerability of Success* 98.

15 "NonEmiratis were 356,343 in 1975 after the first oil boom, thus accounting for 64 per cent of the resident population. Thirty-five years later, in 2010, according to NBS's estimate, their number had multiplied by twenty to an estimated 7,316,073 persons, or 88.5 per cent of the total resident population of 8.3 million" (10). See https://gulfmigration.grc.net/media/pubs/exno/GLMM_EN_2018_01.pdf.

16 See https://www.voltairenet.org/IMG/pdf/Migration_and_the_Gulf.pdf.

17 See https://www.thecommononline.org/who-writes-the-arabian-gulf/#_ftn1; subsequent quotations are from this source.

18 See Bullard to Weir (15 Oct. 1970), National Archives, United Kingdom (NA), FCO8:1540.

19 See John Bonar, "Why Gold Is Too Hot," *Times* (London), (10 Aug. 1975); "Mr. B.S. Abdur Rahman—One Man Many Missions," *Gulf Today* (29 July 2006); "Banks Expand with Growth of Commerce," *Financial Times* (5 June 1969); and "Bangladesh Customs Hit Gold Bonanza in Unlikely Places," *Arab News* (28 May 2017).

20 Todd Reisz notes, "Money, the theory seemed to be, infused place with longevity. Founding the National Bank of Dubai was part of a campaign to pull more banks, and therefore credit to Dubai. . . . The NBD's rise was set within an index

of projects that composed a narrative of a new city built out of the financial optimism the US consulate described in 1964" (193).

21 See https://www.rfz.ae/dubai-health-city-freezone.

22 See "Dubai Transforming to Become Health Center," *Akhbar Dubai* (10 Sept. 1969). Translation by Sandra Bsat.

23 See "Bangladesh Customs Hit Gold Bonanza in Unlikely Places," *Arab News* (28 May 2017).

24 Tomkinson, *The United Arab Emirates* 144.

25 See File 48743, British Petroleum Archive, University of Warwick.

26 See "Dubai Development Plan Review" (May 1971), John R. Harris Library.

27 Todd Reisz notes, "In 1975, Dubai counted twenty-eight banks; Abu Dhabi, sixteen" (267).

28 Zeina Maasri references Deborah Poole's work in *Vision, Race, and Modernity* (1997), where Poole makes the valuable distinction between a "visual economy" and a "visual culture" to argue "for thinking globally about the circulation of images" (17).

29 See DITEC draft press release (n.d.), John R. Harris Library.

30 See "Haunted by Ghost Buildings," *Construction Week Online* (12 June 2010).

31 According to Reisz, "Building schedules were reliant upon competent builders, mostly Pakistanis, who maintained a quality of concrete pours never previously achieved in Dubai" (294).

32 Dubai International Trade Center and Exhibition Center, study prepared by Trizec Corporation, Ltd. (Dec. 1976), John R. Harris Library.

33 Non-nationals (someone not Emirate) need visas or a Residency Permit to live and work in the UAE. The period for legal residencies is generally three to ten years, with an option to renew. Non-nationals can only "buy"

property for a period of ninety-nine years. Otherwise, non-nationals with permits enjoy the same tax-free salaries and health benefits as UAE nationals.

34   See https://www.leisureatemirates.com/aab2b/about-us.

35   Todd Reisz points out that "a major task for the diwan's design team was to figure out how a project—with 16,000 square meters of high-ceilinged office space, chandelier-adorned assembly rooms, a plant compound, more than 300 parking spaces, all surrounded by the surveillance of at least three guardhouses—could fit contextually among what remained of the crumbling Bastakiya district" (328).

36   See https://nrivision.com/can-expats-buy-properties-in-uae/8252/.

37   See Lemos Horta and Robbins, *Cosmopolitanisms*.

38   Asad Haider engages with Paul Gilroy's discussion of blackness and "ethnic absolutism" in Gilroy's 1987 *There Ain't No Black in the Union Jack* (27).

39   See https://market-trends.dandbdubai.com/news/an-architectural-marvel-museum-of-the-future.

40   See https://www.nationalgeographic.com/environment/article/dubai-ecological-footprint-sustainable-urban-city.

41   In "The Cosmopolitan Idea and National Sovereignty" Robert J. C. Young references the German sociologist Ulrich Beck's work in Cosmopolitan Vision (2006), noting that, with Homi K. Bhabha, Beck views institutions such as American universities in the Middle East as an example of a "'both/and' structure of cosmopolitanism which replaces the 'either/or' structure of nationalism" (140–41).

REFERENCES

Albudoor, Khalid. "All That We Have." Gulf Poets Suite, Blackbird Archive, https://blackbird.vcu.edu/v9n2/poetry_gulf/albudoor_k/all_page.shtml.

———. "All That We Have." *Gathering the Tide: An Anthology of Contemporary Gulf Poetry,* edited by Patty Paine, Jeff Lodge, and Samia Touati, 2011, Ithaca P, 2013, pp. 349–52.

Augé, Marc. *Non-Places: An Introduction to Supermodernity,* translated by John Howe, Verso, 1995.

Baudrillard, Jean. "Simulacra and Simulations." *Jean Baudrillard, Selected Writings,* edited by Mark Poster, Stanford UP, 1988, pp. 146–84.

Bhabha, Homi, K. "Spectral Sovereignty, Vernacular Cosmopolitanisms, and Cosmopolitan Memories." *Cosmopolitanisms,* edited by Paulo Lemos Horta and Bruce Robbins, New York UP, 2017, pp. 143–54.

———. *The Location of Culture,* Routledge, 1994.

Bender, Thomas. "The Cosmopolitan Experience and Its Uses." *Cosmopolitanisms,* edited by Paulo Lemos Horta and Bruce Robbins, New York UP, 2017, pp. 120–30.

Davidson, Christopher M. *Dubai: The Vulnerability of Success.* Hurst and Company, 2008.

Haider, Asad. *Mistaken Identity: Mass Movements and Racial Ideology.* Verso, 2020.

Horta, Paulo Lemos, and Bruce Robbins, editors. *Cosmopolitanisms.* New York UP, 2017.

Maasri, Zeina. *Cosmopolitan Radicalism: The Visual Politics of Beirut's Global Sixties.* Cambridge UP, 2020.

Maktoum, Al Bin Rashid. *Spirit of the Union, Lecture on the Occasion of the United Arab Emirates' Fortieth National Day.* Motivate Publishing, 2012.

Marozzi, Justin. *Islamic Empires: Fifteen Cities That Define Civilization.* Penguin Books, 2019.

Mignolo, D. Walter. "The Many Faces of Cosmo-polis: Border Thinking and Critical Cosmopolitanism." *Public Culture.* Duke UP, 2000, pp. 721–48.

Naga, Noor. "Who Writes the Arabian Gulf?" *The Common,* October 5, 2021. https://www.thecommononline.org/podcast-noor-naga-on-who-writes-the-arabian-gulf/.

Poole, Deborah. *Vision, Race, and Modernity: A Visual Economy of the Andean Image World.* Princeton UP, 1997.

Reisz. Todd. *Showpiece City: How Architecture Made Dubai.* Stanford UP, 2021.

Shukla, Ramesh. *The United Arab Emirates: Forty Years of Historical Photographs.* Motivate Publishing, 2011.

Tomkinson, Michael. *The United Arab Emirates*. Michael Tomkinson Publishing, 1975.

Unnikrishnan, Deepak. *Temporary People*. Penguin Books, 2017.

Waldron, Jeremy. "What Is Cosmopolitan?" *Journal of Political Philosophy*, vol. 3, no. 2, 2000, pp. 227–43.

Young, C. J. Robert. "The Cosmopolitan Idea and National Sovereignty." *Cosmopolitanisms*, edited by Paulo Lemos Horta and Bruce Robbins, New York UP, 2017, pp. 137–42.

ABOUT THE COVER PHOTO

The Dubai Frame, completed January 1, 2018, symbolizes the city's transformation from a small port town on the Arabian Gulf into one of today's iconic cosmopolitan cities. Standing as it does between what is known as "old Dubai," or Deira, and "new Dubai," with its skyline of architectural wonders, the steel, glass, and aluminum structure explicitly frames what is said to have been its founding fathers' gaze into the city's future. Merging the visions of Sheikh bin Rashid Al Maktoum, the father of Dubai's current ruler, Sheikh Mohammed Al Maktoum, and that of Sheikh Zayed bin Sultan Al Nahyan of Abu Dhabi, the newly formed United Arab Emirates' first president, The Frame represents the combined ambitions of its founding fathers who were always looking forward. Standing in Zabeel Park at 150.24 meters (493 feet) high and 95.53 meters (313 feet) wide, lore has it that Sheikh Rashid, Sheikh Zayed, and Sheikh Mohammed faced the desertscape with old Dubai at their backs as they imagined the UAE's ever-modernizing potential.

ABOUT THE AUTHOR

 **Adrianne Kalfopoulou** is the author of three poetry collections, most recently *A History of Too Much*, and the prose collection, *Ruin: Essays in Exilic Living*. A collection of poems in Greek, *Xeno, Xeni, Xenia* (translated with Katerina Iliopoulou) was published by Melani Publications.